Engaging Eurasia's Separatist States

Engaging Eurasia's Separatist States

Unresolved Conflicts and De Facto States

Dov Lynch

UNITED STATES INSTITUTE OF PEACE PRESS
Washington, D.C.

UNITED STATES INSTITUTE OF PEACE
1200 17th Street NW, Suite 200
Washington, DC 20036-3011

First published 2004

Printed in the United States of America

The paper used in this publication meets the minimum requirements of American National Standards for Information Science—Permanence of Paper for Printed Library Materials, ANSI Z39.48-1984.

Library of Congress Cataloging-in-Publication Data
Lynch, Dov, 1970–
    Engaging Eurasia's separatist states : unresolved conflicts and de facto states / Dov Lynch.
       p. cm.
    Includes bibliographical references and index.
    ISBN 1-929223-54-4 (pbk : alk. paper)
     1. Transcaucasia—Ethnic relations—Case studies. 2. Ethnic conflict—Transcaucasia—Case studies. 3. Transcaucasia—History—Autonomy and independence movements. 4. Dniester Moldovan Republic—History—Autonomy and independence movements. I. Title.

DK509.L96 2004
320.9475'09'049—dc22

                                 2004041214

Contents

Maps

Foreword

For more than ten years, a group of self-proclaimed states in the southwestern corner of what used to be the Soviet Union have maintained a precarious existence. Unrecognized by the international community, prey to organized crime, mired in economic misery, scoured by ethnic cleansing, and seared by recent memories of war, these hard-pressed territories have clung to their independence, ever fearful that the states from which they seceded will reabsorb them. The fear is not entirely unfounded, for although the metropolitan states (Moldova, Azerbaijan, and Georgia) are currently too weak militarily to retake the breakaway states (Transnistria, Nagorno-Karabakh, Abkhazia, and South Ossetia), they have not abandoned hopes of one day emulating Russia, which recaptured—or at least has reoccupied—its own secessionist territory, Chechnya. How, despite their many weaknesses, these so-called de facto states have endured is one of two central questions posed by *Engaging Eurasia's Separatist States,* a slim but highly illuminating study of the dynamics that sustain both unrecognized states and secessionist conflicts.

The other central question, which comes in two parts, is not only analytically interesting but also distinctly pragmatic in its implications: Should the international community be concerned about these conflicts between post-Soviet metropolitan and de

facto states? And if so, what can the international community do
to stabilize the region? The first part of this question may seem
cavalier or callous, but the answer is by no means self-evident. With
so many other hotspots vying for the attention of the international
community, why should these conflicts merit consideration?
After all, the de facto states are small, with populations no larger
than those of typical small and medium-sized U.S. cities. The conflicts between the separatists and the metropolitan authorities
are not hot; for the most part, cease-fires have held for years.
Moreover, if the parties to the conflicts are themselves apparently
content to see the present state of affairs continue indefinitely,
why should outsiders bestir themselves to intervene?

I will leave it to the reader to discover how Dov Lynch, who
has traveled widely in this beautiful but volatile corner of the world,
answers the first of these questions—about how the de facto states
manage to survive. But I trust the author and reader will forgive
me if I eliminate any suspense surrounding the second question
by noting here that Lynch does indeed think the international
community should concern itself with what happens in this impoverished, underpopulated part of Eurasia. As the author makes
clear, there are in fact several reasons why the international community should care, ranging from the area's strategic importance as a gateway to Europe and a transit point for resources
from the Caspian Basin region and Central Asia, to the billions of
dollars of foreign investment in the local oil and gas industries,
to the fact that the de facto states are breeding grounds and
transit zones for international criminal activities. Moreover, Lynch
not only contends that there are excellent reasons for international concern but also proposes how the international community
might act. He argues strongly for a coordinated approach that
combines "some form of acceptance of the current existence of
the de facto states," "a package of measures—economic, security,
confidence-building, and societal—that support a settlement process," and "political will . . . to shape the various measures taken by
various organizations and states into a more coordinated whole."

My reason for emphasizing this aspect of *Engaging Eurasia's Separatist States* is not only to commend the book's relevance for policymakers as well as scholars but also to illustrate a wider point. Conflicts that seem to be too remote geographically and too quiescent militarily to pose a threat to the wider international community are often more dangerous than they appear. Some conflicts may pose no threats to their neighbors, either near or far, but such conflicts are uncommon. The contemporary world is differentiated from previous decades and centuries not least by its interdependence. Transnational flows of people, information, and business—and of arms, crime, and terrorism—are the norm, not the exception. In such an environment, the temptation to concern ourselves only with the most visible and pressing of crises abroad is understandable, but it is also counterproductive to building national as well as international security.

This is a point made not just in this volume—the research for which was supported by an Institute grant—but in several other publications from the United States Institute of Peace. The Institute has, for instance, just published *Taming Intractable Conflicts*, an eloquent and compelling argument by Chester Crocker, Fen Osler Hampson, and Pamela Aall for the importance of well-crafted third-party mediation in bringing deep-rooted and protracted conflicts to a peaceful close. A similar plea for the international community to involve itself—when circumstances and resources permit—in ostensibly localized conflicts and to craft creative, context-responsive strategies to contain or end the violence is made in books as diverse as Michael Lund's *Preventing Violent Conflict: A Strategy for Preventive Diplomacy;* John Paul Lederach's *Building Peace: Sustainable Reconciliation in Divided Societies;* and *A Strategy for Stable Peace: Toward a Euroatlantic Security Community,* by James Goodby, Petrus Buwalda, and Dmitri Trenin.

The published works of the Institute overlap with the concerns of *Engaging Eurasia's Separatist States* in at least three other ways, too. First, the question of how to satisfy the demands of independence-minded minorities short of secession lies at the heart of Ruth Lapidoth's much-praised volume, *Autonomy: Flexible Solutions to Ethnic Conflicts,* and Tim Sisk's much-cited study, *Power Sharing and International Mediation in Ethnic Conflicts.* Second, just as Dov Lynch focuses on struggles in which ethnic identity plays a central causal role, so too do a host of other Institute authors. Some portray the problems of a specific country, as Rotimi Suberu does in the book *Federalism and Ethnic Conflict in Nigeria;* others paint a much broader canvas, among them Ted Robert Gurr, whose book *Peoples versus States: Minorities at Risk in the New Century* reports on no fewer than 275 politically active ethnic and other communal groups. And third, Lynch is by no means the first Institute author to examine the problems besetting the successor states of the former Soviet Union. To name just a few examples: Martha Brill Olcott has profiled Kyrgyzstan, Kazakhstan, and Uzbekistan in *Central Asia's New States,* Peter Reddaway and Dmitri Glinski have dissected the corruption of Russian politics under Yeltsin in *The Tragedy of Russia's Reforms,* and Anatol Leiven has explored "a fraternal rivalry" in *Ukraine and Russia.*

This breadth of endeavor reflects the Institute's dedication to its congressionally mandated mission—to promote research, education, and training on the peaceful management and resolution of international conflicts—and its determination not to restrict its interest to those conflicts that are currently highest on the media's or the government's agenda. As Dov Lynch reminds us in this stimulating study, in today's world even conflicts far from our shores have a way of endangering our interests and our security.

Richard H. Solomon, President
United States Institute of Peace

Preface

FIFTEEN NEW STATES AROSE from the collapse of the Soviet Union. Recognized by the world and admitted into the club of states, they acquired the protective shield of a body of law developed expressly to protect states, with sovereignty as the foundational norm. International recognition resembles a process of reification; the fifteen post-Soviet states shed their former shapes as union republics of the USSR to become states—the single most important form of political organization in world affairs. If, in past centuries, there existed myriad forms of political organizations—from states to empires, city-states to dependencies—there are few shapes left at the start of the twenty-first century. There are states, and there is little else.

This book provides a new look at the Soviet collapse and the process of state building that erupted across one-sixth of the world's landmass. In addition to the fifteen recognized states, five other "states" declared themselves also independent: Chechnya, Nagorno-Karabakh, South Ossetia, Abkhazia, and Transnistria. The first of these, Chechnya, has since seen its self-proclaimed independence crushed, but the other four have endured, despite being unrecognized and isolated, their very existence deemed illegitimate and unlawful. If considered at all, they are called "badlands" and "criminal dens." The truth is, nobody knows much about them.

This book poses a simple question: How do they survive? How have these entities endured since the Soviet collapse—without international recognition, existing under constant threat, all the while building the institutions of statehood? The question occurred to me when I first visited Transnistria and Nagorno-Karabakh in 1998, and it led me through a research project, funded by the United States Institute of Peace, that ran from 2000 to 2002. This book seeks to answer this question and raises another one: What should the international community do with the unrecognized states? More particularly: How might the principles of self-determination and sovereignty be reconciled? And what approaches could be considered to move toward conflict settlement?

Parts of the research for this book were conducted while I was a visiting research fellow at the WEU Institute for Security Studies in July 2001. The work was completed as a research fellow at the European Union Institute for Security Studies in 2002 and 2003. The initial project was funded by the United States Institute of Peace in the framework of a two-year project titled "De Facto States and Eurasian Security," which I directed at the Department of War Studies, King's College London.

My thanks first go to the United States Institute of Peace for its support to this project since 2000. Nigel Quinney was a constant source of ideas and assistance during the editing process, for which I am very grateful. I also thank the five anonymous reviewers for their comments and queries. I am grateful also to the European Union Institute for Security Studies, and to its director, Nicole Gnesotto, for her advice and support. The Department of War Studies, King's College London, remains an intellectual home for me, and I thank Professor Brian Holden Reid for his help. A number of colleagues have provided rich suggestions on this work at its various stages of development: Roy Allison, Bruno Coppieters, James Gow, Craig Oliphant, Jonathan Cohen, Rachel

Clogg, and Tom de Waal. The numerous trips made to the separatist states would never have been possible without the help of many. In Moldova and Transnistria, I would like to thank Sergei, Igor, Slava, and Dima. In Georgia and Abkhazia, I am grateful to Max and all of the team at the ministry for their welcome and help. In Nagorno-Karabakh, I wish to thank Artemis especially for her kindness and support. There are many others who will remain unnamed, but I am no less grateful for their allowing me to question them about their dreams. Finally, I wish to thank Eric Baudelaire, *mon compagnon* on many of these travels. This book is dedicated to Francesca Maria Devalier for everything that is, and to Caspar the magnificent.

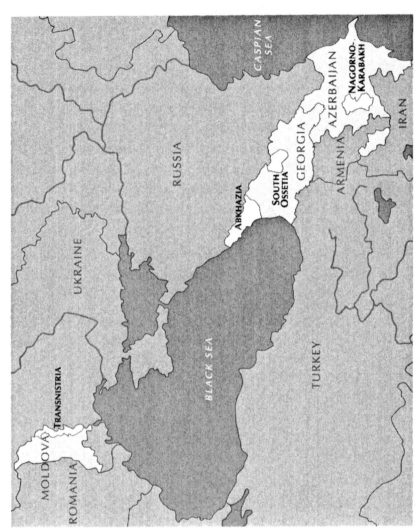

Moldova, Georgia, Azerbaijan, and Neighboring States

Moldova and the Pridnestrovyan Moldovan Republic (Transnistria)

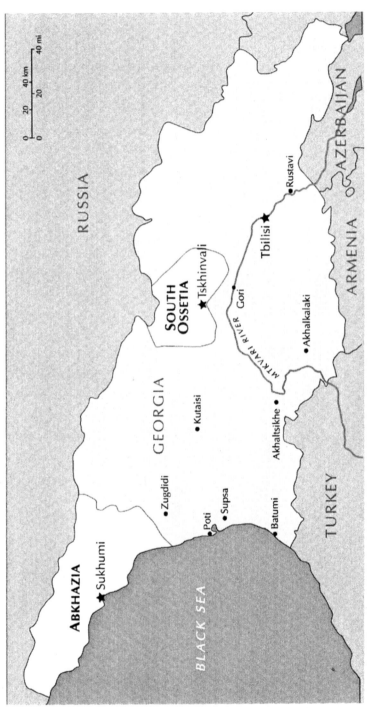

Georgia, the Republic of South Ossetia, and the Republic of Abkhazia

Azerbaijan and the Nagorno-Karabakh Republic

Engaging Eurasia's Separatist States

1

Introduction

A MAP OF THE WORLD provides the onlooker with a sense of completion: the globe has been divided up into legally equal sovereign states, and all territories and peoples fall under one or another of these units' jurisdiction. The world is a complete matrix of colors and lines that leaves nothing to chance. The blank spots have been filled in. The map of the former Soviet Union conjures a similar satisfaction. Fifteen new states emerged from the Soviet collapse. All of the territory has been divided up and formal jurisdiction claimed across all of the post-Soviet space.

This satisfaction is misplaced. In late November 2000, the city of Tiraspol, formally under the jurisdiction of the Republic of Moldova, held an unusual summit.[1] It brought together the foreign ministers of four separatist regions that have declared independent statehood in the former Soviet Union: the Pridnestrovyan Moldovan Republic (PMR or Transnistria) inside Moldovan borders, the Republic of South Ossetia and the Republic of Abkhazia, both within Georgian borders, and the Nagorno-Karabakh Republic inside Azerbaijan.[2] The foreign ministers agreed to create a permanent forum called the Conference of Foreign Ministers to coordinate the activities of their separatist governments. They also discussed a blueprint for the settlement of the conflicts that they face. The blueprint called for the recognition of "sovereign equality" between the separatist regions and the authorities in Moldova, Georgia, and Azerbaijan (hereafter referred to as the metropolitan states) as the only path leading to conflict resolution. There had been similar meetings of the separatist governments in the early 1990s, none of which had much impact on the conflicts. This summit, too, was unlikely to have dramatic effect.

The summit did, however, perform a service in highlighting an enduring but often forgotten reality of security in the post-Soviet space. In addition to the fifteen successor states that emerged in 1992, four other "states" exist that are unrecognized.[3] (A fifth unrecognized state, Chechnya, is, as of this writing, virtually nonexistent and thus is not examined in this volume.) These separatist states are not found on any map of the former Soviet Union. They are isolated in international relations, and they all face deep internal problems and existential external threats. If ever discussed, the separatist areas are typically dismissed as criminal strips of no-man's-land or as the puppets of external states. There has been much analysis devoted to individual cases of conflict in the former Soviet Union; however, there has been no full comparative study of the separatist states.[4]

Two works—one by Edward Walker, the other by Charles King—have come near to such a study. Edward Walker's long, path-breaking article published in February 1998 focused on three "secessionist conflicts" in the Caucasus: Abkhazia, Nagorno-Karabakh, and Chechnya.[5] His argument was heavily descriptive and considered the conflicts one after the other. His basic point was that a situation of "no peace, no war" had developed in each of the conflicts that was founded on the military success of the secessionist movements, the imposition of cease-fire regimes favorable to them, and the lack of progress in talks, driven by a reluctance on any side to reach compromise. The article had a wealth of detail on each conflict and painted a clear picture of the status quo. However, the work was not fully comparative, and little attention was devoted to drawing out the social, political, and economic forces sustaining the status quo. Nor did Walker analyze the foundations of the state-building projects initiated by each of the secessionist parties. In concluding, Walker posited that comprehensive settlements were far off in these conflicts: "The best that can reasonably be hoped for are staged agreements in which both sides agree to disagree on status while building trust through limited agreements on specific issues." This important conclusion was not developed further.

Charles King addressed all four extant separatist states in a July 2001 article in *World Politics*.[6] King placed his analysis of the cases of Abkhazia, South Ossetia, Transnistria, and Nagorno-Karabakh in the context of wider research on how to end civil war, arguing persuasively that an "equilibrium" had been reached in each of these conflicts and concentrating on the role of the state-building projects as a critical factor behind the status quo. The equilibrium is driven by a number of factors, namely, the construction of states in the secessionist regions, the weakness of the central government and its collusion with the status quo, and the role of external actors, including Russia, diasporas, and even international organizations. In the end, King argued, "just as the political economy of war can perpetuate violence, so too the institutions of Eurasia's unrecognized states have ensured that the benefits born of conflict continue to accrue to belligerents on both sides, the erstwhile losers as well as the winners." King's analysis was illuminating in many ways, but it was not complete in its discussion of the forces driving the separatist states to insist on sovereignty. The thrust of King's analysis was analytical and not prescriptive. Still, he noted in conclusion that recognizing the existence of the separatist states may be the only obvious solution to these conflicts, provided the separatist entities remain within the formal structures of the recognized states. The article finished on a qualified note, however, with King stating that this might prove too difficult for "new, fragile and allegedly democratizing states."

The current study draws on the work I have undertaken since 2000 on the post-Soviet "de facto states."[7] In articles published in 2001 and 2002, I concentrated mainly on analyzing the

factors behind the inertia that had developed in all of these conflicts due to the existence of the separatist states. This study presents a more complete analysis of the social, political, economic,
and military forces sustaining the stalemates in the post-Soviet
conflicts and, on this basis, discusses ways out of the impasses.

Cease-fire agreements have been reached in all the separatist areas. Internationally led negotiations have been under way
in all of them since the early 1990s. In the conflicts in Moldova
and Georgia, Russian/Commonwealth of Independent States
(CIS) peacekeeping forces have been deployed to maintain a
buffer zone between the conflicting parties. The United Nations
and the Organization for Security and Cooperation in Europe
(OSCE) have also become deeply involved in mediating in these
conflicts, as well as in monitoring the activities of the CIS peacekeeping forces. However, since 1992 there has been little progress
toward settlement. The de facto states are the main reason for
the absence of progress.

From the perspective of the international community, does
the continuing existence of the de facto states pose any significant
problems? Do they threaten international security? Given that
active combat has stopped in these conflicts, why should the international community care what happens to the de facto states?

At the most fundamental level, the fact that these conflicts
have not been resolved does not pose an existential or direct
threat to wider international security. However, the international
community, and certainly Europe, no longer has the luxury of
considering only existential threats. As the very notion of security has become deeper and wider, the existence of unresolved
conflicts in the European and Caucasian regions of the former
Soviet Union cannot be ignored. There are strategic interests in
these areas. Moldova, squeezed between Romania and Ukraine,
represents the outer rim of the Balkan area and an eastern gateway
for Europe. Georgia is a strategically important transit country
for the passage of goods and especially energy resources from the
Caspian Basin region and Central Asia. Azerbaijan has become

the focus of billions of dollars of investment by European and U.S. oil companies seeking to exploit the vast potential of that country's reserves in oil and gas.

The separatist states have an impact on the security of the states from which they have seceded—the metropolitan states—and on wider regional developments. Close to two million people have been displaced by these wars, putting serious strain on the new states of Moldova, Georgia, and especially Armenia and Azerbaijan. The economies of these new states are all deeply affected by the existence of the unrecognized states. The self-declared states have presented external powers with opportunities to intervene in the region. Russia has used its peacekeeping operations in Moldova and Georgia as means to retain influence over those two states.[8] Conditions within the de facto states have exacerbated problems of organized crime in the post-Soviet space. The legal limbo in which they exist has made them breeding grounds and transit zones for international criminal activities. Most importantly, the use of force has remained an option in all the post-Soviet secessionist conflicts, as the renewed fighting in Chechnya since August 1999 has shown.

If the existence of the de facto states does matter for international security, the next questions are these: What approach should be taken to move these conflicts toward some kind of settlement? More specifically, what sort of endgame is realistic in these conflicts?

The de facto states of PMR in Moldova, South Ossetia and Abkhazia in Georgia, and Nagorno-Karabakh in Azerbaijan have existed for more than a decade. While limited in the grand sweep of history, ten years is not negligible. These conflicts are often called "frozen," as little progress has occurred toward their resolution. Yet, while the cease-fire lines have not changed and remain frozen, in most other ways the word "frozen" is misleading. The concept of a dynamic logic is a more fitting way of understanding why there has been no conflict resolution, for much has happened in these areas over the past ten years. This logic has both external and internal dimensions. Any movement toward settlement must take into account this logic, and any settlement will have to focus more on the structures that have developed over the past decade and less on the original sources of the conflicts.

The conclusions of this study are relevant to the wider discussion on the notion of "ripeness" as a prerequisite for conflict settlement.[9] Ripeness corresponds with a moment in a conflict after escalation when the conflicting parties have reached a position of mutually hurting stalemate and seek to attenuate the pain of maintaining the status quo through negotiation. The argument made in this study qualifies this concept as it might be applied to civil wars between central governments and separatist regions. Painful stalemates have been reached in all the post-Soviet conflicts. The status quo carries costs for all the parties, in terms of social-economic difficulties and political burdens. However, in the past decade all the conflicting parties have developed internal structures and external sources of support that offset the pain of stalemate. For the separatist states, the status quo crowns their achievements on the battlefield and their de facto independence, both of which are salves to the difficulties that they face from being unrecognized by the international community and living under blockade. The metropolitan states have also developed mitigating strategies that offset the pain of the current stalemate. The status quo hurts, but is does not hurt everyone in the same way and it does not hurt enough to force a settlement.

The use of armed force is one solution for dealing with the de facto states. The use of force by the Russian Federation to quell its separatist region of Chechnya (the self-declared Republic of Ichkeria) in the North Caucasus is one example of this approach. Beyond the forceful solution, however, is a range of other options by which to move these conflicts toward settlement—all of which accept the continuing existence, in one form or another, of the de facto states. The international community has good reasons not to recognize these separatist states, but it also has the opportunity to support a solution that lies between the extremes of recognition and elimination. The de facto states of PMR, Abkhazia, South Ossetia, and Nagorno-Karabakh and the metropolitan states of Moldova, Georgia, and Azerbaijan could survive without conflict settlement, but none of them will prosper.

This study examines the internal and external dynamics driving the continuing existence of the separatist areas. Chapter 2 clarifies a number of important conceptual issues, defining the concept of a de facto state and describing the context that facilitated its emergence in the former Soviet Union. Chapter 2 also sketches brief histories of the four de facto states. Chapter 3 examines the forces that drive the de facto states, focusing on the political, military, and economic logic that underpins the separatist states at the internal and external levels. The fourth chapter discusses the security impact of the de facto states on the metropolitan states and regional developments.

Chapter 5 explores ways out of the current volatile impasse. The analysis examines the approaches taken thus far by the international community toward these conflicts and proposes an alternative that may help to break the inertia of a decade of entrenched conflict. In seeking to balance the norm of territorial integrity with the right to self-determination, the alternative proposed here has relevance to other conflicts that present a similar dichotomy of separatist and metropolitan states, such as those in the former Republic of Yugoslavia. A proposal for a new approach to the conflict in Moldova is sketched out in some detail.

Most fundamentally, this study argues that settlement is possible only if it is premised on some form of acceptance of the current existence of the de facto states. International recognition need not be attributed to them; however, the existence of extensive independence in these areas must be recognized. This recognition must be combined with a package of measures—economic, security, confidence-building, and societal—that support a settlement process. Settlement of these conflicts requires a balance between de facto and de jure sovereignty and independence. The aim here is not to develop a comprehensive blueprint that can be applied to each conflict. They are all sufficiently different that this would be a vain ambition. The central point is that of coordination: if the various strands of conflict settlement are not coordinated and interwoven, or if one or several are lacking, a settlement process is likely to unravel, as was witnessed in the case of the Nagorno-Karabakh conflict in 2001. The costs for the international community in addressing these conflicts are not high in material terms, whether in the form of money or the deployment of military forces. The cost lies in the realm of political commitment: political will is required to coordinate the existing strands of policy already undertaken by the international community, to shape the various measures taken by various organizations and states into a more coherent whole. For now, current international approaches, lacking coordination and strategy, work against one another and thus sustain the status quo. The central objective must be to break the inertia by adopting a coordinated approach that takes account of the current conflict system and seeks to alter its key points.

The research for this study is based on several months of travel and interviews on the ground in the conflict zones in 2000, as well as shorter visits before and after 2000.[10] The focus of the research is on the PMR in Moldova, Nagorno-Karabakh in Azerbaijan, and Abkhazia and South Ossetia in Georgia. In discussing Georgia, this study concentrates mainly on Abkhazia, rather than on South Ossetia, because the Abkhaz case has been far more volatile and entrenched, and the Abkhaz separatist state has proceeded further on the path of state building independently of Georgia. Nonetheless, the argument draws on the example of South Ossetia whenever appropriate.

This study does not consider in detail the case of the de facto state in Chechnya, the Republic of Ichkeria, now almost nonexistent and in an active state of war with the Russian federal government. After the first war between 1994 and 1996, the question of Chechnya's status was suspended by agreement of all parties at Khasavyurt for a period of five years. The Chechen authorities sought to enshrine the independence of the region from Russia after this accord and aspired to be recognized by the international community as a full-fledged member. In some respects, therefore, the Republic of Ichkeria was a de facto state in the interim period between 1997 and 1999, sustained by a combination of internal and external forces similar to those examined in the following chapters. The movement of Russian troops into the republic in October 1999 put an end to the de facto status, plunging the region into an ongoing conflict. This study focuses on those states where empirical research on the ground has been feasible. The analysis concentrates also on those areas that have benefited from cease-fires since the early 1990s and on de facto states that have proceeded much further than Chechnya in developing the institutions of statehood. This does not mean that the example of Chechnya between 1997 and 1999 does not offer parallels to the separatist states under review here.[11] Simply put, the concentration falls on those areas that have successfully endured nonrecognition for over ten years.

The main objective is to draw out the main forces driving the separatist entities in the former Soviet Union by using the region's most prominent cases. The aim is not to present an exhaustive analysis of all cases of separatist states in international affairs, nor does this work seek to clarify debates about the origins of conflicts in the former Soviet Union. The argument does not present a blow-by-blow account of developments in these conflicts. Moreover, while presenting a general definition of de facto states and the place of these entities in international affairs, and while considering parallels with other examples of separatist states in Europe and beyond, the argument here does not have wider theoretical ambitions.

A final note concerns the potential for bias in the research and analysis. The lion's share of the fieldwork for this study was conducted within the separatist states, for the simple reason that the voices of the inhabitants of these areas have been largely ignored for the past decade in most discussions of the conflicts.

The fact that many interviews drawn upon in this study are with individuals in the de facto states reflects not a political bias in their favor but simply the desire to explain more clearly a point of view that is generally unheard. Moreover, calling these separatist areas "states" does not amount to an argument for their recognition but rather draws attention to the essential obstacle to conflict settlement, which is the state-building projects these areas have undertaken.[12] These post-Soviet conflicts have displaced close to two million people, and tens of thousands have been killed. While all suffer, a key point made in this study is that many profit also. The objective is not to distribute blame or recrimination, but to understand more clearly.

2

The De Facto State
Definition, Environment, and Emergence

DEFINING THE DE FACTO STATE

Before defining the concept of de facto states, it is helpful to start by considering a conflict in the former Soviet Union that has been settled. In June 1997, a peace agreement ended a vicious civil war in Tajikistan. Why was settlement possible in Tajikistan while it has failed in Moldova, Georgia, and Azerbaijan? The Tajik settlement throws light on the sticking point in these other post-Soviet conflicts and lays the ground for a clear definition of the concept of the de facto state.

The Tajik civil war provoked many statements about the threat it posed to regional stability.[1] The civil war had devastating results, with an estimated 20,000 to 40,000 victims, 600,000 internally displaced persons (IDPs), and at least 100,000 refugees.[2] However, a peace process has advanced in Tajikistan following the General Agreement of June 1997. Since then, changes have been made to the Tajik constitution. Formally at least, opposition armed forces have started to be integrated into the national armed forces. IDPs, as well as some 50,000 refugees in northern Afghanistan, resettled in Tajikistan with the support of the United

Nations and the OSCE. While flawed, new presidential and parliamentary elections occurred in November 1999 and February 2000. Islamic figures of the United Tajik Opposition were appointed to high-level posts in the government, leading to formal power sharing with the conservative regime in Dushanbe under President Emomali Rakhmonov. This progress toward conflict settlement is unique in the former Soviet Union.

Why has settlement been possible? The answer to this question is simple but revealing: It was a civil war and not a war between two parties claiming to be states (even if only one party is legally to be considered a state).

The civil war in Tajikistan featured a contest over power in the new state. By 1996, the United Tajik Opposition sought a share of power in Dushanbe, and a weakened President Rakhmonov recognized the need to compromise with his armed opponents. Most importantly, the Tajik civil war was not a conflict over the nature of the Tajik state, its borders, or its makeup. While containing an ideological dimension, the fundamental "idea" behind the new Tajik state went unchallenged. The conflict also lacked the ethnopolitical dimension characteristic of other post-Soviet conflicts. The common ground between the parties is founded, however weakly, on a sense of shared history and destiny that has allowed progress to occur in power sharing and the resettlement of IDPs and refugees.[3]

In contrast, the armed conflicts in Abkhazia, South Ossetia, Transnistria, and Nagorno-Karabakh reflect conflicting perceptions of the domain and scope of the territory of the new states of Georgia, Moldova, and Azerbaijan. (The same can also be said of Chechnya and Russia.) The aim of the separatist groups is not to capture power in the capitals of the metropolitan states or to renegotiate the division of state powers within a given territory. The objective is to *exit* the metropolitan state. The aim is to build new relations with it as an equal unit. The linkage of ethnicity with territory has made the objectives of the separatist areas state oriented—nothing less than sovereignty will suffice for their authorities. This disagreement about the "idea" behind the new states of Moldova, Georgia, and Azerbaijan has made conflict resolution along the lines set in Tajikistan difficult, if not unattainable. In this light, it may be worth seeing these not as civil wars but as interstate wars. The difference between the Tajik civil war and the other post-Soviet conflicts may seem obvious. However, many of the settlement proposals put forward by the international community during the 1990s were based on some form of power sharing—not dissimilar to the Tajik model. Such solutions are unlikely to be effective in the case of secessionist conflicts.

In the first monograph-length theoretical examination of de facto states, Scott Pegg defined them as follows:

> A de facto state exists where there is an organized political leadership, which has risen to power through some degree of indigenous capacity; receives popular support; and has achieved sufficient capacity to provide governmental services to a given population in a specific territorial area, over which effective control is maintained for a significant period of time. The de facto state views itself as capable of entering into relations with other states and it seeks full constitutional independence and widespread international recognition as a sovereign state.[4]

To understand the de facto state, points must be made. First, Pegg's definition is based on a distinction between empirical and judicial notions of statehood. The de facto state is not recognized by other states or the international community. As a result, it has no judicial status in the international arena. The de facto state has no judicial right to claim a certain territory, as this land already is part of a recognized state. However, it may have an empirically defined claim to statehood. The classic definition of an entity that may be regarded as a sovereign state was set forth in the Montevideo Convention on Rights and Duties of States of 1933. The Montevideo criteria are that an entity have (1) a permanent population, (2) a defined territory, (3) a government, and (4) the capacity to enter into relations with other states. The

post-Soviet de facto states fulfill the first three of these criteria
and claim to pursue the fourth. However, the empirical qualifi-
cations of the de facto state cannot make it legal or legitimate in
international society. As Pegg argued, it is "illegitimate no matter
how effective it is."[5]

Second, it is necessary to distinguish between internal and
external sovereignty. Internal sovereignty refers to the supreme
authority of a body within a given territory.[6] External sovereignty
may be defined as "being constitutionally apart, of not being contained, however loosely, within a wider constitutional scheme."[7]
The de facto state claims both to be sovereign over its territory
and people, and to be constitutionally independent of any other
state. The key difference for the de facto state resides in its nonrecognition. This status prevents it from enjoying membership
in the club of states—the de facto state does not have recognized
external sovereignty.

STATES AND SOVEREIGNTY

De facto states have arisen from what Robert Jackson called the
"new sovereignty game."[8] This game started with the process of
decolonization during the Cold War and has consisted of a regime regulating the emergence of new states, the criteria of self-
determination, and the conditions for international recognition.[9]

The UN General Assembly Resolution 1514 (Declaration
on the Granting of Independence to Colonial Countries and
Peoples) of December 14, 1960, set forth many of the rules of
the current regime. The declaration stated that all peoples have
the right to self-determination and to determine freely their political status and forms of political, economic, and social development. The resolution established juridical statehood as the basic
norm for the granting of sovereignty to an entity. The lack of any
form of empirical "preparedness" was deemed not a valid reason
for denying independence. As a result, self-determination became a legal and moral right to all non-self-governing territories

that are distinct from the country that administers them (following the so-called salt water criterion). In the critical words of Michael Freeman, the application of these rules meant that the putative right to self-determination became "ossified by the anticolonial idea, the Westphalian consensus, and *uti possedetis juris,*" the principle that newly decolonized states inherit the colonial administrative borders they held at independence.[10] On this point, it is important to distinguish between the *principle* of the right to self-determination, which is overarching, and the *rules* for its application, which were limited to colonies.[11] The UN declaration denounced "any attempt aimed at the partial or total disruption of the national unity and the territorial integrity of a country."

This informal regime sought to mitigate the potentially explosive effects of decolonization and the creation of new states by enshrining both a limited notion of self-determination and a juridical definition of criteria for new states. Self-determination was to occur only once, at the moment of decolonization. *Uti possedetis juris* was sanctified to ensure stability through an insistence on absolute territorial integrity and equal sovereignty. The rule was also expanded to include intrastate sovereignty: self-determination by all peoples was out of the question, and secession was condemned outright. The constant border changes and state territorial shifts that had been the fabric of international affairs until the middle of the twentieth century were condemned as illegal and disruptive to order. Most profoundly, these rules meant that the new states that emerged from decolonization could not *fail;* they could be weak, even nonexistent on the domestic and international scene, but they could no longer disappear. Somalia is a case in point.

This freezing of the territorial map had two effects that are supportive of the emergence of de facto states. First, the right to self-determination has remained an overarching principle with pride of place in moral terms in international affairs. Stanley Hoffmann took his cue from Kant in noting, "Justice itself requires that the right be granted, for there is no more certain injustice than alien rule imposed against the will of the people."[12] On this point, James Mayall argued that "this unprecedented attempt to bring history to an end, at least so far as the territorial division of the world is concerned, seems unlikely to succeed" as long as the pursuit of this form of justice in popular self-determination remains widely held.[13] International relations have remained underpinned by principles that militate against a strict interpretation of *uti possedetis juris*. The clash between the pragmatic and the moral universe has created scope for regions, peoples, and areas within states to seek self-determination as part of what they consider the universal pursuit of liberty.[14]

Second, the areas seeking self-determination face an incentive system that leads them to seek statehood rather than any other form of existence—autonomy or association—with their metropolitan state. The absolute nature of state sovereignty as it has emerged since the 1960s has diluted international society of all the gradations between types of entities that had existed previously. The international game is now closer to zero-sum; there are states and there is little else. The exclusive nature of the club of states, and the principles of equal sovereignty and of noninterference upon which it is based, has meant that most self-determination movements will be content with nothing less than state sovereignty to achieve what they perceive as justice.

And for good reason. Recognized sovereignty is a source of vitality for states.[15] It provides a range of opportunities for protection and self-defense, and it embeds the state firmly in the international society, guarding against the possibility of extinction.[16] The principles of territorial integrity, equal sovereignty, and the norm of nonintervention constitute the "societal fabric of international relations" as well as unique sources of strength for states.[17] Without state sovereignty and its recognition by the international community, a separatist movement has very few rights and no status that protects it in international law. The extermination of a separatist movement through the use of force by the metropolitan state cannot be ruled out. The separatist state is not protected by the rules governing the legal state regime, and it lacks the vitality that recognized sovereignty provides. This system pushes a separatist area toward the pursuit of full state sovereignty.

EXAMPLES OF DE FACTO STATES

In 1984, Alan James argued that "jurisdictionally speaking there is never any doubt about where one stands and that one always stands on the domain of a single sovereign state."[18] In a jurisdictional sense, James is correct. However, the legal freezing of the map that has occurred since the end of World War II has not wiped away all areas claiming to be states but lacking the legal recognition of their sovereignty by the world community. De facto states do exist.

They include the Republic of China (Taiwan), which has existed since the end of the Chinese civil war and has survived being recognized and then derecognized by the main actors in the international community. Despite the refusal of the People's Republic of China to recognize Taiwan, the small island has become deeply engaged in world affairs and the world economy and has also secured the security assistance of the United States. Moreover, Taiwan participates in a number of international fora and has developed "privatized" diplomatic representation abroad despite nonrecognition. Another example is that of Eritrea, which launched a struggle against Ethiopian rule in 1961 and fought from small clashes to full-scale military operations for thirty years. The civil war left hundreds of thousands dead, produced three-quarters of a million refugees, and ravaged the country. Eritrean military victories led the Ethiopian government under President Meles Zenawi to start the process of fully recognizing Eritrean sovereignty.[19] This process culminated with the UN-monitored referendum on independence of April 1993, where 98.5 percent of more than a million Eritrean voters cast their ballots for independence. For long periods after the late 1970s, most Eritrean lands were under the control of the Eritrean People's Liberation Front, and the region was run as a de facto state that was able to put in the field not only a powerful military force but also significant administrative capacities. In his analysis, Pegg cited the view of one expert on the conflict that by 1984 "the EPLF was already stronger and better organized than many governments in Africa."[20]

Examples of less successful de facto states are more common than Taiwan's economic success story or Eritrea's path to political victory. In such cases, territories within recognized states have formed separatist structures and declared independence but remain unrecognized by the international community— even if the recognized state barely exists in reality. The Republic of Somaliland, a former British colony, in the northern part of Somalia, a former Italian colony, is a case in point.[21] In the words of William Reno, "Somaliland authorities preside over a hybrid organization—not exactly a state in a conventional sense—but state-like in the more basic sense of preserving order, as a pole around which citizens establish a shared identity, and manage the community's conduct of relations with outsiders, all integral elements of self-determination."[22] The development of de facto state capabilities in Somaliland must be understood in contrast to the collapse of Somalia as a viable state by the early 1990s. In her analysis, Peggy Hoyle raised a pertinent question: "How can Somaliland be condemned for seceding from Somalia if there is no Somalia from which to secede?"[23]

The Turkish Republic of Northern Cyprus (TRNC), declared after the partition of the island of Cyprus in 1974, presents similarities with the post-Soviet de facto states. The TRNC has not received international recognition, while the Greek-dominated Republic of Cyprus enjoys all the benefits of such recognition.[24] Since partition, the TRNC has developed, with the support of Turkey, all of the empirical attributes of state capacity despite its isolation. Population displacement has played an important role in the conflict. The current status quo reflects a durable cease-fire line that is based on clear military realities and the recognition that the TRNC will not be overrun by force. Moreover, the TRNC benefits from the support of an external patron state, which has alleviated the pain of nonrecognition. Finally, the long-standing involvement of the international community, mostly through the United Nations, in seeking to reach a settlement has produced few results despite decades of work.

For all the similarities with the TRNC and others, the Eurasian de facto states have several unique features. They were all born in the dying days of the Soviet Union and reflect the particular nature of politics in the USSR before and during its collapse. As discussed below, the administrative structure of Soviet federalism played an important role in the rise of the de facto states. Moreover, the USSR was very much a garrison state, which made military equipment and training widely available to all parties throughout the Soviet Union. Linked to these factors, the former Soviet Union contains an unusually large number of de facto states. Fifteen states joined the United Nations in 1992, but there were at least five unrecognized states declared or in the making, stretching from Nagorno-Karabakh to Chechnya. Moreover, Russia has played a critical role in all of the separatist states, as mediator-cum-supporter-cum-combatant. Finally, the rise of the post-Soviet de facto states coincided with the end of the Cold War and the acceleration of various processes of globalization. The end of the Cold War has seen an increasing role attributed to the United Nations and other international organizations in seeking to settle regional and local conflicts. Nongovernmental organizations have also assumed far greater responsibilities in the conflict zones than they had in the past. The rise of financial and economic globalization has meant the erosion of strict state control over flows to and from their countries and created a propitious climate for de facto states to develop ties with various diaspora groups, as well as criminal organizations, beyond their borders.

THE SOVIET COLLAPSE AND THE RISE OF POST-SOVIET DE FACTO STATES

The end of the Cold War saw the emergence of local and ethnic conflicts in Europe and beyond, which stimulated a number of debates about the sources and nature of ethnic conflict. Discussions of the conflicts in the former Soviet Union reflected these wider debates. Some scholars emphasized the role of insecurity as a driving force behind the wars that erupted.[25] In these views, the Soviet collapse tended to produce perceptions of insecurity from various groups and the generation of a security dilemma, in a context of easily accessible weapons and opening political space for popular participation. In contrast, Stuart J. Kaufman stressed the role of the "symbolic politics of ethnic war" as a key factor.[26] In his discussion of the conflicts in Georgia and Moldova and over Nagorno-Karabakh, Kaufman identified the three conditions for ethnic war as the existence of myths justifying hostility, the prevalence of fears, and the opportunity to mobilize and fight. The combination of these conditions, in his view, tended to produce mass hostility, to exacerbate the politics of extreme nationalism, and to feed a vicious security dilemma. Still others have examined the role of particular factors in the origins of the post-Soviet conflicts. Svante Cornell, for one, analyzed the role of the Soviet federal autonomy structures as a factor that exacerbated other driving forces in these conflicts, such as radical leadership, past conflict, geography, and demography.[27] In his discussion of the Tajik civil war, Barnett Rubin examined the role of economic dislocation and the struggle for economic survival as a factor driving conflicts in a collapsing state with an ethnically and regionally heterogeneous population mix.[28] Increasingly, the trend in the scholarly literature is toward less theory and more empirical research on the origins and course of conflicts in the former Soviet Union. Thomas de Waal's work on Nagorno-Karabakh is an excellent example of this trend.[29]

The Soviet Collapse

In addition to the general pressures in the international system, described above, three factors specific to the Soviet legacy help explain the emergence of de facto states. First, the peculiar nature of Soviet federalism helped shape understandings of ethnicity and power in the late 1980s and 1990s across the post-Soviet space. Stalin had linked the nation with ethnicity and territory in *Marxism and the National and Colonial Question*.[30] In the Soviet Union, ethnicity was territorialized and tied to institutions and different levels of representation, resulting in a state that was indeed "national in form and socialist in content."[31] The Soviet territorialization of ethnicity had several effects. Soviet federalism, argued Ronald G. Suny, reinforced a "making-of-nations" process that had started across the region in the pre-revolutionary period.[32] Suny noted that "rather than a melting pot, the Soviet Union became the incubator of new nations."[33] In this sense, the Soviet collapse was not a thaw that allowed the awakening of nations long slumbering under the sedative of coercive Soviet communism—these nations had been long awake. However, the reforms initiated by Gorbachev allowed political space for the genuine representation of ethnicity and nationalism and also stimulated elites to seek ethnic and national legitimacy as a form of popular mobilization.[34] The legacy of the Soviet experience was that group rights had to be *territorialized* to mean anything. The legacy was also that formal structures had to be created for the recognition of the existence of a group and the protection of its autonomy.

Second, Soviet federalism was based on different levels of regionally and ethnically based administrative units. These levels conferred different status and power, with the union republics at the apex of the system, which contained autonomous republics, autonomous regions, and autonomous areas. This experience discredited for many who had lived in the Soviet system the notion of autonomy as a valid institution for the protection of a group's rights.[35] De jure, the republics/regions/areas had autonomy, but real power resided elsewhere, with the union republics and Moscow. The legacy from this was paradoxical. Structures of autonomy supported the territorialization of ethnicity. However, the experience of autonomy was often negative for members of the titular nationality in the autonomous structure, who were well aware that power lay elsewhere. It was also negative for the titular nationality in the union republic in which the autonomy was embedded, who saw it as means of Soviet/Russian "divide and rule."[36] Thus, in Georgia, the Georgian elites in Tbilisi resented the autonomous rights given to the Abkhaz in the Abkhaz autonomous republic inside Georgian territory, interpreting this as a means by which Moscow weakened Georgia. At the same time, the autonomous Abkhaz were discontented, being well aware that Tbilisi had final word on most decisions and that autonomy meant very little.

As the Soviet Union collapsed, the uncertainties inherent in this situation became exacerbated and a spiral of insecurity ensued. For the autonomies, such as Abkhazia, South Ossetia, and Nagorno-Karabakh, the Soviet experience led to an emphasis on moving beyond autonomy to a higher status as the only solution to guarantee their existence and the protection of their rights. The existing structures of autonomy gave these peoples ready-made institutions to wield against the capitals of the metropolitan states in which they lived; elected parliaments, executive agencies, police forces, universities, and all the trappings of sovereignty were mobilized in the pursuit of independence.[37] For their part, the former union republics of Georgia and Azerbaijan typically sought to maintain the Soviet "autonomous" structures as mechanisms of control over rebellious ethnic groups. (The Soviet structures were discarded in the case of South Ossetia, which had its autonomy abolished.) Whereas elsewhere in Europe the delimitation of autonomous structures within states has helped to assuage conflicts, the result was the opposite in the former Soviet Union: the existence of autonomous structures exacerbated conflicts.[38]

Third, the process by which the new states of the former Soviet Union were recognized by the international community also stimulated the separatist movements. Recognition was attributed to the "highest" units in the Soviet Union, the union republics, following the lines set by the decolonization model of attributing juridical recognition to already existing entities with the support of the former imperial power.[39] Recognition of the Baltic republics went particularly smoothly as the international community had never recognized formally their incorporation into the USSR. The eleven other union republics, except Georgia, which was then in internal turmoil, were recognized soon after the demise of the USSR (recognition of the Republic of Georgia followed in March 1992). The process enshrined the rule of *uti possedetis juris* and the principles of the UN Charter and the Conference on Security and Cooperation in Europe (CSCE, now the OSCE) on territorial integrity and respect for existing borders. However, it left the autonomous structures inside the new states vulnerable to the new nation- and state-building projects occurring around them. The Abkhaz, the Ossets, and the Karabakh Armenians found themselves all of a sudden citizens of states dominated by Georgians and Azerbaijanis.

As argued by Jirair Libaridian, former state adviser to the first Armenian president, Levon Ter-Petrosyan, the international community then placed its bets on formal stability in the region and sought to reassure the autonomous entities that continued existence within the new states would be positive.[40] According to Libaridian, the premise underlying the recognition process was that the new states of Moldova, Georgia, Azerbaijan, and Russia would pursue democratization and economic reform that would benefit *all* peoples within the new international borders. Thus, the rights of minority areas and peoples would be defended and the drive to separatism would be abandoned.

The autonomous entities saw these promises of democracy and prosperity as empty. The recognition process as a whole was regarded as arbitrary and, worse, as deeply unjust. The perception of local actors was that the boundaries of the union republics had been drawn up by Moscow following the principles of political expediency and divide and rule, not with any consideration for the long-term viability of these units. In fact, many of the inner borders seemed designed to build fragility into these entities. The borders of Armenia and Azerbaijan, with ethnic enclaves in Nakhichevan (Azerbaijani dominated) and Nagorno-Karabakh (Armenian dominated), are a case in point. Soviet policies also divided ethnic groups across different republics. The conflict over the status of South Ossetia in Georgia finds much of its source in the fact that neighboring North Ossetia is an autonomous republic within the Russian Federation, while South Ossetia was an autonomous region within Georgia. For the Abkhaz, Ossets, and Armenians, it proved a step too far for them to accept the long-term promise of prosperity while, in the short term, they were fighting active conflicts with the metropolitan states. Far from being a recipe for stability, the recognition of new international borders in 1992 was one ingredient of conflict.

Perestroika had a catalyzing effect in each of the conflicts. The collapse of the centralizing and coercive power of the Communist Party, combined with the introduction of glasnost and limited free elections, allowed new political arenas to open, which became theaters in some cases for nationalist and ethnic mobilization. The ongoing dislocation of the Soviet economy accelerated pressures for locally driven reform strategies. This situation was the context for the conflicts that arose in the late 1980s in Georgia, Moldova, and Azerbaijan. The transformation of the Soviet system initiated by Gorbachev was the central conditioning factor in all of these conflicts, whether mass-led, as in the case of Nagorno-Karabakh, or elite-led, as in the Transnistrian case. The ingredients were similar in each case. Systemic transformation opened new space for political activity and mobilization, which decreased the risk of repression and produced further disarray, which in turn stimulated further popular mobilization and fear, all in the context of a heavily militarized state, in which weapons were readily available and Soviet/Russian troops were scattered throughout disparate parts of the empire with less and less ability to control events. In the words of David Laitin and Ronald Suny: "By any definition, this was (and continues to be) a period of revolutionary transformation. It was simultaneously a tale of the dismantling of a leviathan state and the replacement of old forms of state and economic power with the partial construction of fragile new state authorities."[41]

The Separatist Conflicts

GEORGIA-ABKHAZIA. The Georgian-Abkhaz conflict has a distinctly ethnic character.[42] The roots of the conflict lie partly in the Soviet period.[43] After 1917, the region of Abkhazia maintained a relationship of treaty association with Georgia, until it was incorporated as an autonomous republic within Georgia in 1931. By 1989, the Abkhaz represented only 17.8 percent of the autonomous republic's population. As Georgian nationalism flourished in the late 1980s, the Abkhaz population, and especially a section of the local elites, became increasingly restive, fearing their possible cultural and ethnic disappearance within Georgia. Both parties had developed rich historical visions of the legitimacy of their claim to control this land during the decades before Gorbachev's arrival in power.[44] Moreover, the history of Georgian-Abkhaz relations had not been free of tension in the twentieth century, especially during the first Georgian Republic (1918–21) and in the 1920s and 1930s. In March 1989 several thousand Abkhaz signed the Lykhny Declaration, organized by the People's Forum of Abkhazia, which called for the creation of a Soviet Socialist Republic of Abkhazia, separate from the Georgian Union Republic. Armed clashes broke out in July 1989, after the Georgian attempt to create a branch of Tbilisi University in the Abkhaz regional capital, Sukhumi. As Soviet central power waned, Abkhaz leaders became fearful of the growing strength of Georgian nationalism and Tbilisi's political power. In response, Abkhaz leaders maintained a pro-union stance in the face of Georgian moves toward independence. Following the collapse of the Soviet Union, this stance shifted toward one of independence from Georgia.

Interethnic relations grew more tense after Zviad Gamsakhurdia's success in the October 1990 presidential elections in Georgia. Gamsakhurdia adopted exclusive state-building policies that alienated the minorities in the country, starting with the South Ossetians (see below). In July 1991 Gamsakhurdia negotiated a compromise electoral law for the Abkhaz region that guaranteed the Abkhaz a strong position in the local soviet (twenty-eight seats were allocated to the Abkhaz, twenty-six to Georgians, and eleven to other nationalities). This compromise was rejected by numerous Georgian politicians living in Abkhazia, as well as by political elites in Tbilisi.

Gamsakhurdia's nationalizing and personalistic policies led to the emergence of a Georgian opposition in Tbilisi. His suppression of student demonstrations in Tbilisi in September 1991, after his ambiguous stance on the August coup in Moscow, led to the coalescence of opposition forces. The conflict took the form of clashes between paramilitary and independent armed groups, which assumed substantial political power in such turbulent times. The head of the National Guard, Tengiz Kitovani, went over to the opposition. The paramilitary group Mekhedrioni (Horsemen) also rallied to the opposition's cause. After armed clashes in Tbilisi, Gamsakhurdia went into exile in January 1992. A Military Council, composed of Tengiz Sigua, Tengiz Kitovani, and Jaba Ioseliani, invited Eduard Shevardnadze to return in March 1992. Shevardnadze's hold on power was tenuous, as he faced powerful figures in the council with control over independent militias. Moreover, Gamsakhurdia retained support in the western regions of Georgia. At the same time, the Abkhaz autonomous region was moving toward greater independence under the leadership of Vladislav Ardzinba, a former academic colleague of Yevgeny Primakov's from Moscow and former deputy to the USSR Congress of Peoples' Deputies. In July 1991, the Abkhaz parliament declared that Abkhazia would revert to its 1925 constitution, which described Abkhazia as an independent Soviet Republic united by a special union treaty with Georgia.[45] Conflict erupted in August 1992, after Georgian forces entered Abkhazia, expecting to restore Georgia's territorial integrity quickly.

The war turned out differently. At first, Georgian forces— really a ragged mix of government troops and militias—repulsed the Abkhaz authorities from Sukhumi and even landed on the northern coast of Abkhazia. The Abkhaz regrouped in the autumn of 1992 in the town of Gudauta and, with the support of volunteers from the North Caucasus and with Russian arms, forced back the Georgian bridgehead in the north. Russia was an important source of support to the Abkhaz cause in the form of both matériel and the participation in combat of Slavic officers and troops.[46] A surprise Abkhaz offensive in September 1993, three months after a cease-fire and withdrawal had been agreed to under loose Russian supervision, expelled all Georgian forces from the Abkhaz region. Over the course of the thirteen-month war, several thousand people were killed and hundreds of thousands of Georgians were displaced from their homes in Abkhazia.

The front line between Georgia and Abkhazia has not changed since 1994. Following a cease-fire agreement in May, Russian peacekeeping forces under CIS aegis were deployed in June 1994 along the Inguri River separating separatist Abkhazia from metropolitan Georgia proper. The initial peacekeepers were drawn from the ranks of Russian forces already in the conflict zone. On the ground, these forces have done little to halt constant low-level skirmishes in the border zone of the Gali district, where thousands of Georgian IDPs have trickled back. Many of the IDPs were swept out again in May 1998 by an Abkhaz offensive to rid Gali of Georgian paramilitary forces. The United Nations deployed the United Nation Observer Mission in Georgia

(UNOMIG) in 1994 to observe and monitor the activities of the CIS peacekeeping forces and developments in and around the security zone. In addition, the United Nations has led negotiations between the two parties since 1994, but progress has been largely formal: no settlement on the status of Abkhazia has been reached, the IDPs have not returned to their homes, skirmishing continues in and around the security zone, and Abkhazia remains under trade restrictions imposed by Georgia and the CIS. Since the early 1990s, the Abkhaz authorities, under the leadership of President Vladislav Ardzinba, have proclaimed independence from Georgia and set out to develop all the institutions of statehood, despite nonrecognition and international isolation.

GEORGIA–SOUTH OSSETIA. The South Ossetian Autonomous Region had been included in the Georgian Republic in 1922, separating it from the Autonomous Republic of North Ossetia, within the borders of the Russian Republic. In November 1989, the Supreme Soviet of the South Ossetian region voted to upgrade its status to the level above that of a region—to autonomous republic, still within the Georgian Republic. Occurring at a moment of heightened and exclusive Georgian nationalism, the event provoked a swift reaction by Tbilisi; the decision was revoked. Following a year of tension, the new Georgian parliament annulled South Ossetian status as an autonomous region, a downgrading that precipitated an armed conflict between Georgian forces and the small region on the border with Russia. South Ossetia consisted on four districts with a capital town of Tskhinvali and a population in 1989 of some one hundred thousand (of whom 66 percent were Ossets, 29 percent Georgians, and the remainder a mixture of Russians, Armenians, and even Greeks). The war caused significant physical damage and forced the displacement of an estimated sixty thousand people, mainly Ossets, who crossed to North Ossetia. Fighting lasted until June 1992, when a ceasefire was agreed to and a trilateral peacekeeping operation deployed, led by Russian forces.

Since 1992, the cease-fire regime has held firmly, and relations between the Georgian and the Osset communities have been normalized, with contacts and transportation links being restored. The OSCE and the European Union have sponsored a number of confidence-building programs, but these have had little effect on the settlement of the question of South Ossetia's status. Despite economic weakness, deep criminalization (from smuggling across the Russian border), and political instability, South Ossetia declared its independence as a sovereign republic and has built formally all the structures of statehood. Presidential elections in the self-declared republic in November 2001 were won by Eduard Kokoyev, who has since pursued an unwavering course of independence. One reason for the lack of progress in the settlement of the South Ossetian conflict is that it is seen to depend on the resolution of the more violent and deeply entrenched struggle between Tbilisi and Abkhazia.

MOLDOVA-TRANSNISTRIA (PMR). The conflict between the central authorities of Moldova and the separatist region of Transnistria started in the late 1980s as the Moldovan Soviet Socialist Republic distanced itself from Moscow.[47] When the Moldovan Union Republic declared independence from the Soviet Union on August 27, 1991, its only previous claimed period of independence had been in the fifteenth century under Prince Stephen Cel Mare, whose death was followed by centuries of external domination of Moldova. In 1538, Moldovan lands fell under the control of Suleyman the Magnificent, and the Dnestr River became one of the outer frontiers of the Ottoman Empire. The land east of the Dnestr—that is, present-day Transnistria—had a different history. It was only in 1812 that the two regions were brought under the control of the same power, Russia. The two areas were divided again when Romania recaptured Bessarabia in the chaos of the Russian Revolution. Briefly, after the incorporation of Moldova into the USSR under the terms of the Molotov-Ribbentrop pact, the Transnistrian region was transferred from

Ukrainian to Moldovan jurisdiction in 1940.[48] The German invasion of the USSR made this arrangement irrelevant. Soviet troops in 1944 swept through the left bank (i.e., the east bank) and across the Dnestr, repulsing the German and Romanian armies, and the two banks were joined again as the Moldovan Soviet Socialist Republic within the Soviet Union.

The recent conflict erupted in the late 1980s with language as its first battleground. Transnistria had lived through the tumult of the early years of Soviet rule between 1918 and 1945, but the right bank had been spared this under Romanian rule. With the creation of the Moldovan Union Republic in 1945, the right bank was "sovietized" in short order, with agriculture collectivized and elites at all levels purged.[49] Moreover, the Soviet authorities rewrote the history books to declare the uniqueness of Moldova and its non-Romanian identity.[50] The Moldovan language was said to have different roots than its Romanian twin, and to prove this, Moldova's Latin alphabet was changed to the Cyrillic. Institutions were created—schools, universities, and teaching colleges—to produce a new Moldovan (non-Romanian) elite and nation, ruled from the capital, Chisinau.

In the late 1980s, an umbrella group called the Moldovan Popular Front rose to challenge this Soviet policy, campaigning for a shift from the Cyrillic back to the Latin script.[51] Language laws to this effect, adopted in August 1989, led to strikes across the left bank. As with the Abkhaz case, the leaders in the Transnistrian region maintained a staunch pro-union position in the hope of countering any increase of power in Chisinau that might lead toward greater Romanian influence and undermine their political and economic power. In Moldova, the collapse of the Soviet Union resulted in a contest over the identity and orientation of the new state. The call by parts of the Popular Front for an eventual Moldovan reunification with Romania was a sore point for the highly sovietized and russophone population across the Dnestr; authorities and factory directors of the left bank increasingly appealed to conservative forces in the Soviet center.

The conflict was, therefore, ethnically driven to the degree that the language issue and the prospect of reunification with Romania aroused fears in the left-bank population, including its Moldovan component.[52] Nonetheless, the roots of the conflict were political and economic.[53] Under Soviet rule, the Moldovan Union Republic had been governed by elites from the Transnistrian region.[54] In the 1980s, a new generation of leaders from Bessarabia rose to challenge Transnistrian predominance. Combined with this, Moldova's movement toward political and economic independence threatened Transnistrian control of local industries and, especially, the subsidies that the factories on the left bank received from Moscow. In the words of Charles King, by the late 1980s the people on the Dnestr River "were living in two increasingly distinct worlds"—the right bank was more "Moldovan" and more agricultural, while the left was "sovietized" and more industrial.[55]

Throughout the autumn that followed Moldova's declaration of independence, Transnistrian militias sought greater control over the towns and villages in the left bank. Sporadic violence and clashes continued into 1992. As King states, "every move in Chisinau that pulled the republic farther away from Moscow was met by a countermove in Transnistria that drew the region itself farther away from Chisinau."[56] The active period of combat reached its height with a struggle over the town of Bendery in June, where a group of Transnistrian forces, including volunteer Cossacks and with the support of the Russian 14th Army, routed Moldovan police forces. In all, close to a thousand people were killed.

The lines of the conflict have remained unchanged. By bilateral agreement between the two conflicting parties, a peacekeeping operation was deployed in a security zone that follows the Dnestr River. The operation is Russian led and composed of Russian troops as well as Moldovan and Transnistrian battalions. The Russian Operational Group (formerly the 14th Army), deployed on the left bank of the Dnestr, assumed peacekeeping responsibilities in the security zone in mid-1996. Its makeup is predominantly local, which has meant a significant degree of support, especially among the officers, for the Transnistrian case throughout the 1990s.[57] The Moldovan government has sought the withdrawal of Russian forces in accordance with the bilateral agreement of October 1994. At the Istanbul summit of the OSCE in November 1999, the Russian government agreed to withdraw its forces and, more importantly, its massive weapons stocks by late 2002. This deadline was then put off until late 2003. In fact, very little progress has occurred.

The OSCE deployed a long-term mission in Moldova in April 1993.[58] Part of its mandate has been to monitor the activities of the peacekeeping operation and the security zone. The OSCE reached an agreement, the Principles of Cooperation between the OSCE Mission and the Joint Control Commission in the Security Zone, on July 20, 1994 (updated on January 16, 1996). These principles allow it to patrol the security zone and participate in the Joint Control Commission.[59] According to members of the OSCE mission, the Transnistrian delegation, and not the Russian one, has obstructed significant OSCE monitoring— forcing the mission to remain silent in Joint Control Commission meetings and preventing the mission from visiting Transnistrian "border" posts.[60]

Since the cease-fire, negotiations have taken place between the two parties under the aegis of the OSCE, and a number of protocols have been agreed to.[61] Under Russian pressure, led by then foreign minister Yevgeny Primakov, the two parties agreed to the Memorandum on the Basis for Normalization of Relations between the Republic of Moldova and Transnistria in May 1997. This agreement stipulated that the two parties would build future ties within the framework of a "common state" consisting of the territory enclosed by Moldova's borders as they stood in January 1990. Further progress has been held up by different interpretations of the notion of the common state. A draft settlement "non-paper" put forward by the OSCE in 2002 called for Moldova's federalization, with the attribution of significant autonomy to Transnistria.[62] Despite external pressure, the Transnistrian authorities were reluctant to accept this draft as a basis for negotiations but agreed in 2003 to a joint commission with Moldovan experts to rewrite the Moldovan constitution. Over the past decade, the Transnistrian authorities have consolidated their control over the left bank, creating all the institutions of statehood and exercising a significant degree of control of Transnistria's self-declared territory.

AZERBAIJAN–NAGORNO-KARABAKH. The conflict between Azerbaijan and the separatist region of Nagorno-Karabakh began with a long and vicious war that started in the late 1980s.[63] Twenty-five thousand people died in the war and over seven hundred thousand people, mainly Azerbaijanis, were displaced, forced from Nagorno-Karabakh and the surrounding Azeri districts. In May 1994, the Russian government brokered a cease-fire agreement, which has been largely respected. In December 1991, the Armenian authorities in the regional capital of Stepanakert proclaimed an independent Republic of Nagorno-Karabakh, unrecognized by the international community, including neighboring Armenia. Although both Azeris and Armenians have put forward ancient claims to the land of Nagorno-Karabakh, the conflict has modern roots that lie with the rise of Azerbaijani nationalism and Armenian nationalism in the nineteenth century and their evolution under Soviet rule. In the words of Thomas de Waal: "In untangling the roots of the Karabakh conflict, we should first of all dismiss the idea that this was an 'ancient conflict.' Both the form and the content of the Armenia-Azerbaijan dispute date back little more than one hundred years."[64]

The birth of modern Azerbaijani nationalism occurred in the late nineteenth century, largely in reaction to Russian imperial policies in the Caucasus.[65] This nascent nationalism was limited to educated circles in the main towns. Some of these elites came from Karabakh, and from its main town of Shusha, and thus the region was woven into the story of Azerbaijan's national

"awakening." Russia's arrival in the Caucasus had already strengthened the Azerbaijani sense of ownership over Karabakh. The first
Russian-Persian war was followed in 1805 by Russia's annexation
of the khanate of Karabakh. The khanate was abolished and the
Russian *guberniia* of Elizavetpol was created, joining Karabakh with
the Azerbaijani plains to its east. Thus, from 1805 on, Karabakh
was tied to Azerbaijani lands.

From the Armenian perspective, Karabakh has been regarded as Armenian land since the seventh century BC, and the
region has been seen as the exception to the rule that the history of Armenia is the history of a "martyr nation."[66] Whereas
the rest of the Armenian nation had been constantly subjugated
to external powers, Armenian "sovereignty" survived—the Armenians claim—in the Karabakh mountains. Karabakh was captured
by Russia in 1805, but the rest of the Caucasian Armenian lands
were not seized from Iran until 1826.

In Armenia, Soviet rule is seen to have laid the ground for
the current conflict. The Bolshevik leaders initially seemed to
promise to unite Karabakh with the new Soviet Armenian Union
Republic. A resolution of the Caucasian Bureau in Moscow on
July 4, 1921, confirmed the transfer. But a leader of Soviet Azer-
baijan, Nariman Narimanov, protested the proposed union. On
July 5, after barely twenty-four hours of Armenian "unity," Moscow
declared that Karabakh would remain a part of Azerbaijan, "with
wide regional autonomy."[67] In July 1923 Moscow created the
Autonomous Region of Nagorno-Karabakh inside the Azerbaijan
Union Republic. From then on, Karabakh was an enclave inside
Azerbaijan, where an Armenian majority, then some 94 percent
of the local population, was ruled from Baku and cut off from
Armenia. Under Soviet rule, ties between Nagorno-Karabakh
and Azerbaijan became stronger, particularly in economic and
infrastructural terms. In demographic terms, the population of
the region stood at 188,000 by 1989, of which 145,000 were
Armenian and 40,000 were Azerbaijani.[68]

In August 1987, tens of thousands of Armenians signed a petition calling for Karabakh's transfer from Azerbaijan to the Armenian Union Republic. The first violence occurred in October 1987 and the first deaths in Askeran in February 1988. Gorbachev tried to quell these demands with promises of more investment in Karabakh, a heavier dose of cultural autonomy for the local Armenians, and even a period of direct rule from Moscow. But he refused to countenance the transfer of Karabakh to Armenia. On February 21, 1988, the Soviet Politburo rejected the demand for a transfer. In Armenia, a Karabakh Committee was created in early 1989 to spearhead the upsurge of nationalism.

The rise of such a forceful Armenian nationalism, then mostly directed against Moscow, could not fail to affect Azerbaijan. The reaction had two faces. One was blind popular violence. Blood was spilled in the Azerbaijani city of Sumgait, where riots raged for two nights in late February 1988. Sumgait marked the start of a massive exodus of Armenians from Azerbaijan and Azerbaijanis from Armenia, a tidal wave of people driven by fear that accelerated with the start of full-blown war in 1991. A second face was the Azeri Popular Front, a broad-based movement created in 1989 that crystallized Azeri nationalism and led the struggle against Armenia.

All-out war between Armenia and Azerbaijan erupted as the Soviet Union collapsed in late 1991. Azerbaijani troops moved into former Soviet positions inside Karabakh, and Azerbaijan imposed a blockade on Karabakh, cutting off the region from Armenia. Armenian forces counterattacked in the spring and opened a corridor through the town of Lachin, linking Nagorno-Karabakh with Armenia. Azerbaijani forces launched a major offensive in late 1992, but with little success. Throughout 1993, Armenian forces repulsed Azerbaijani forces from the districts that surrounded Nagorno-Karabakh, causing a massive displacement of the Azerbaijani population. The cease-fire that was struck in May 1994 fixed the lines of the conflict. Since then, the authorities in

Nagorno-Karabakh have set about building an independent state, drawing on the institutional resources of its previous autonomous regional stature and tapping the support of Armenia and the Armenian diaspora, all the while facing an economic blockade from its former main economic partner and existing without international recognition.

■ ■ ■

Significant similarities exist between these conflicts. First, in each case, cease-fire agreements have held more or less firmly since 1992–94. These agreements enshrine the victory of the separatist forces on the battlefield and are monitored by a variety of international actors, including Russian peacekeeping forces in Moldova and Georgia. These missions are territorially constrained: that is, the domain of their activity follows a clearly marked security zone that divides separatists from the metropolitan state territory. Over the past decade, founded on the separatist military victory, the military weakness of the metropolitan governments, and the existence of "border" or observer missions, an important degree of stability has emerged on the ground (albeit with some notable exceptions). Second, while settlement talks have been launched in each conflict by international organizations and with the participation of the parties and important third states, there has been no progress on the fundamental question of relations between the separatist areas and the metropolitan states. In this sense, very little normality has been restored between the conflicting parties despite a decade of relative stability on the ground—relations remain constrained, sometimes nonexistent, and little movement has occurred on any side toward public recognition of the legitimacy of other views. Finally, the separatist entities have used the past decade to pursue state-building projects, reflected in the creation of an array of institutions and the development of a discourse of statehood and sovereignty among their elites and populations. For all their weakness, de facto states have emerged in each of these areas. This new reality did not exist at the time of the Soviet collapse.

3

The Logic Driving the Separatist States

THERE ARE TWO PIECES OF CONVENTIONAL WISDOM about these conflicts that require rethinking. The first piece is that external factors are the key obstacles to conflict settlement. The parties themselves are quick to blame external forces for everything—from creating the conflict in the first place to holding off its resolution. Vasily Sturza, then the Moldovan presidential envoy to the negotiations with the PMR, made the point bluntly in July 2000: "The resolution of the conflict depends exclusively on the Russian Federation. Transnistria is an unrecognized state invented from nothing, invented by Russia. Without Russian political and economic support, this invention would not have been possible."[1] Similarly, Tamaz Nadareishvili, the chairman of the Abkhazia parliament-in-exile in Tbilisi, argued in August 2000 that all the post-Soviet conflicts were not civil wars but really "military-political conflicts between these new states and Russia."[2] Russian forces played a key role in the initial phases of these conflicts, and ambiguity in Russian policy has done nothing to help resolve them since. The "Russia factor" permeates these conflicts, with Moscow involved at all levels and in myriad ways. In general, external factors—such as the Russian role or the role of the diaspora—have been, and continue to be, critical barriers to conflict settlement.

However, external forces are not the only ones feeding the status quo. The balance of analysis needs to be redressed. This study concentrates first on the internal forces that inhibit conflict settlement. These political, ideological, military, and economic dimensions present formidable obstacles to settlement. It is the combination of internal drivers with external forces that sustains the status quo. To analyze either internal or external factors in isolation, as is often done, is to obfuscate rather than clarify.

The second piece of conventional wisdom concerns the oft-repeated view that these are "frozen conflicts." They may appear frozen, in that little progress has been achieved in negotiations and the conflicts remain fixed on cease-fire lines established in the first half of the 1990s. In reality, however, the metaphor is misleading—these conflicts are not frozen. On the contrary, events have developed dynamically, and the situation on the ground today is very different from the context that gave rise to these conflicts in the late 1980s. A new reality has emerged since the imposition of cease-fire regimes in 1992–94. The central objective of this study is to examine this new reality. A clearer understanding of the current situation, and the logic sustaining it, is fundamental for thinking about ways to move beyond the impasse.

INTERNAL DRIVERS

There are three internal factors driving the continuing existence of these de facto states: the insistence on absolute sovereignty, a potent sense of fear and insecurity, and the strength of criminal and military elements under weak governments that are trapped in a "subsistence syndrome."

Absolute Sovereignty

The authorities of the de facto states insist on their absolute sovereignty. The amalgam of territory, population, and government in these areas has produced something greater than the sum of its parts—a deeply felt belief in their sovereignty. Vladimir Bodnar, the chair of the Security Committee of the parliament of the PMR, put it most plainly: "We are an island surrounded by states. . . . What defines a state? First, institutions. Second, a territory. Third, a population. Fourth, an economy and a financial system. We have all of these!"[3] The de facto states draw on two legal sources of legitimacy to justify their claim to statehood and two historical-moral sources.

First, these authorities explicitly adhere to an empirical definition of statehood and sovereignty along the lines of the 1933 Montevideo Convention. They maintain that they fulfill all the conditions of positive sovereignty. Vladislav Ardzinba, the Abkhaz president, stated in an interview in November 1999: "Statehood doesn't need to be recognized by the international community. It is sufficient if it is declared by the people themselves."[4]

Each of the de facto states may be said to have—as in Pegg's definition—a system of organized political leadership that has received popular support and that provides basic governmental services to a given population over a specific territory, over which effective control is maintained for a significant period of time. There are numerous similarities between the de facto states at this level. For example, they all maintain presidential systems and have (very poorly developed) party structures. In all of them, while there may be significant political differences, politics is far from pluralistic. The notion of a "loyal opposition" has been long in taking root in the de facto states. The very idea of an opposition is controversial in states under siege. Nonetheless, a loyal opposition has emerged in each of these de facto states. In Abkhazia the war veterans' group, Amstakhara, has placed increasing pressure on the ailing Ardzinba to cede power.[5] Opposition politics emerged earlier in Nagorno-Karabakh as a result of the tensions between civilian and military authorities, and particularly between the separatist president and the former defense minister.

In general, politics is highly personalized and the mechanics of the decision-making process are opaque and highly controlled. The path taken by the president of South Ossetia, Eduard

Kokoyev, is a case in point. Kokoyev was elected in November 2001 with the support of the powerful Tedeyev brothers, Albert and Jambulat. On July 1, 2003, Kokoyev fired his military aides and dissolved the special military units that had been under the control of the two brothers.[6] The dismissal of the Tedeyev brothers from formal positions in the separatist government has done little to relieve their pressure on Kokoyev. But it does highlight the importance of politically and economically powerful individuals as driving forces in the de facto states.

A lack of political transparency is common to all these areas. This is particularly so in the PMR, where the Ministry of Security has a strong presence in the media and politics, so as to undermine any opposition to President Igor Smirnov. In all of the de facto states, parliamentary and presidential elections have occurred periodically since 1991, which have been monitored by "observers" from the other separatist states. And all of them feature heavy state censorship in the televised and written media. The degree of popular support for their leaders and policies is difficult to assess in all of them because elections have been controlled. In the 1999 Abkhaz presidential elections, the only candidate to run was the incumbent, who won an overwhelming majority of the popular vote.

However, the post-Soviet cases also show variation. The level of governmental service is vastly different from one de facto state to another. At one extreme, the Abkhaz government maintains the daily running of legislative, executive, and judicial institutions but performs very few governmental services for its population. The United Nations and international nongovernmental organizations, such as Acción Contra la Hambre, the International Committee for the Red Cross, and Médecins Sans Frontières, have become the pillars of social security in Abkhazia. The Abkhaz Ministry of Health is little more than a facade for the support of the vulnerable and ill provided by these international organizations. The money brought into Abkhazia by international humanitarian organizations is far larger than the declared budget of the separatist state. Moreover, the Abkhaz state is unable to provide for law and order across its claimed territory. The border region of Gali in the security zone is riddled with crime and armed gangs. Further inside the separatist state, the situation is better but still not far from lawless. The analysis of Alexandre Kukhianidze is insightful: "De facto, the government in Sukhumi is not able to control the territory of the Gali district and the Kodori Gorge and prevent activities of different (Abkhaz and Georgian) crime groups. Frequent assassinations and kidnappings became the usual practice in this region."[7]

The war between Abkhazia and Georgia in 1992–94 occurred solely on Abkhaz territory and left the area devastated, its infrastructure destroyed, and its businesses and industries looted and plundered. The minister of economics, A. Lushba, speaking in 2000, noted that "estimates from the government are that eleven billion dollars is required to rebuild and to restore damage to houses, enterprises, and infrastructure."[8] The Abkhaz education system is struggling for survival in conditions of postwar destruction and endemic poverty. Ten years after the end of the war, the streets of the capital, Sukhumi, remained as they stood after the Abkhaz assault of 1993 expelled Georgian forces: ravaged and derelict.[9]

The PMR and Nagorno-Karabakh are much stronger. In both of them, a sense of state presence is palpable: the streets are lit at night, most of the buildings in the capital town have been rebuilt in the case of Nagorno-Karabakh, and there is no feeling of lawlessness. But they have not been spared the difficulties of transition experienced by all the newly independent states since the Soviet collapse. These difficulties include a collapse of industrial production, widespread hidden unemployment, and the deep impoverishment of their populations. Nagorno-Karabakh has suffered from the severing of trade links with Azerbaijan, its main partner in the Soviet era, and has been swamped by agricultural goods from Armenia, shaking an already destitute agricultural system. Nagorno-Karabakh has floated on the buoyancy provided by diaspora assistance since the end of the war in rebuilding the devastated region, and the separatist budget survives on loans from the Armenian government.[10] Nevertheless, a decade later, the separatist authorities face deep structural weaknesses in terms of limited investment, agricultural collapse, deindustrialization, and widespread impoverishment.[11] The PMR inherited a stronger industrial base than the other de facto states and has been attempting to make the most of its strategic position as an important transit zone for all sorts of smuggled goods.[12]

All of the separatist states have experienced depopulation since the end of the wars. The exodus has touched mostly the other ethnic groups within their borders (the Russians and the Greeks in Abkhazia) and youth, who have left for economic reasons. Moreover, the populations have aged in each of the de facto states. The ratio of workers to pensioners is alarming as a result, with an estimated 1.5 workers for every pensioner in the PMR.[13] The official number of pensioners in Abkhazia stands at fifty thousand, all of whom survive without government support and thanks to family networks and international humanitarian organizations.

Before the war, the ethnic Abkhaz accounted for 17.8 percent of the population of the Abkhaz autonomous region, while the plurality were ethnic Georgians (around 45 percent). As a result of the fighting, some 250,000 Georgians have been displaced from their homes and now live in temporary accommodations throughout Georgia. The exact size of the remaining population of Abkhazia is deeply contested and politically sensitive, as demography resides at the heart of the conflict. The estimates range from about 80,000 to 145,000. Whatever may be the exact figure, the fact remains that Abkhazia is largely depopulated. It is also clear that the ethnic Abkhaz population does not have a clear majority even with the Georgians expelled, as there remains a substantial Armenian and Russian population.

The size of the population of Nagorno-Karabakh is also unclear, with estimates ranging from the unofficial figure of 80,000 to the official count of 185,000. In response to this situation, the Karabakh government announced a nativization program in 2001 to increase the population to 300,000 within a decade. Demography is less of a problem in the PMR, where the population stands at around 650,000, representing a notable but hardly dangerous drop from 1992 levels.

Finally, the degree of state control over territory is also variable. Abkhazia maintains very weak control over its territory. The government has no control at all over some areas, such as the Gali district, and it does not have a monopoly on the use of force inside the country, where every man is armed, Russian troops are deployed, Georgian paramilitary groups remain active, and the ethnic Svans have retained control over the upper Kodori valley. Again, the PMR and Nagorno-Karabakh are much stronger in this respect, with distinct armed forces structures, police agencies, border troops, and customs representatives.

Despite the variations in strength, the separatist governments all insist that their empirical structures are robust enough to enable them to declare state sovereignty. Following the empirical logic of the Montevideo Convention, the chairman of the parliament of the PMR, Grigory Maracutsa, affirmed "Pridnestrovye is a sovereign and independent state."[14] Moreover, the separatist leaders favor the declaratory over the constitutive approach to understanding the recognition of an entity as a state by other states.[15] These governments maintain that recognition does not *create* a state but rather *reflects* an existing reality. The attribution of statehood arises from the empirical existence of sovereignty and not its juridical recognition by other states. As a result, formal recognition of their independence by the international community is seen as secondary for these governments.

On this point, the PMR presents an interesting twist. On several occasions, it was pointed out to me that recognition by the international community was viewed as a status that may in fact complicate the PMR's sovereignty. Vladimir Bodnar argued:

> Recognition gives a state the possibility to work officially
> with other states, and international financial institutions, but
> it is still debatable whether recognition is most useful for a
> state. It provides a guarantee that a state will not be attacked
> in principle. But it also leads a state to honor international
> law and international agreements. From a juridical point of
> view, it is impossible to require a de facto state to do so.[16]

In Bodnar's view, maintaining the status quo of nonrecognition
may better preserve the sovereignty of the PMR. Living in limbo
is profitable for the PMR elites.

The second source of legitimacy claimed by the de facto
states draws on the right of self-determination. On July 25, 2000,
Sokrat Jinjolia, the chairman of the Abkhaz parliament, stated:
"We are independent. We have passed an act of independence.
Nonrecognition does not matter."[17] All the de facto states base
their claims to independence on popular elections or referenda
and legislative acts to this effect.

In addition, the authorities claim legitimacy because of the
way the independence of the metropolitan state was declared. In
the words of Sergei Shamba, the Abkhaz foreign minister: "In
leaving the Soviet Union, Georgia de facto reneged on all the resolutions passed in Soviet times, which became illegal"—including
those which had subordinated the Abkhaz region to the control
of Tbilisi.[18] Georgia's declaration of independence, in the separatists' view, opened the legal avenue for their own declaration.
The separatist authorities in Tiraspol seized upon the resolutions by Moldova's parliament on the illegality of the Molotov-
Ribbentrop Pact in the summer of 1990. To them, this decision
meant that the Moldovan Soviet Socialist Republic that emerged
from World War II was illegal. The point is again technical but
relevant. Before the war, the left bank of the Dnestr River had
been an autonomous republic within the Ukrainian SSR. Therefore, on this basis, in September 1990, the Supreme Soviet of the
left bank passed a declaration of sovereignty and independence.
In addition, referenda were organized throughout the left bank,

and in the town of Bendery on the right bank, to provide popular legitimacy to the Supreme Soviet's declaration.

The de facto states also have approved new constitutions that enshrine what are seen as popular and democratic resolutions on independence and sovereignty. For example, the Abkhaz constitution, approved in a referendum in November 1994, states that the Republic of Abkhazia is a "sovereign democratic state based on law, which historically has become established by the rights of nations to self-determination." In an interview in August 2000 the deputy chairman of the Karabakh National Assembly, M. Okhanjanian, argued also along these lines: "Nagorno-Karabakh is a fully fledged state with all its attributes. In December 1991, we had a referendum on independence; 99.58 percent voted in favor. On the 25th of December, we had the first elections to National Assembly, followed by elections on April 25, 1995, and June 18, 2000, and we had also two presidential elections. All of this shows that we have all the attributes of statehood."[19] Popular will is held up as a pillar of legitimacy to support the separatist states' claim to independence.

There are two further claimed sources of legitimacy: one historical, the other moral. Appealing to history, the de facto states claim that their current incarnation represents but the latest phase in a long tradition of statehood. Sergei Shamba placed great stress on this: "Abkhazia has a thousand-year history of statehood since the formation in the eighth century of the Kingdom of Abkhazia. Even within the framework of empires, Abkhazia kept this history of stateness. No matter the form, Abkhaz statehood remained intact."[20] In this statement, the meaning of sovereignty is just the opposite of the empirical justifications also claimed by these states. Sovereignty here is an idea that does not need to have an institutional form.

For these authorities, history is a useful resource in the struggle to justify the present and establish claims for the future. The current Abkhaz state claims a primordial past and a solid historical foundation, with disregard for the paucity of evidence actually available. Similarly, the PMR authorities hark back to their experience of "statehood" as an autonomous region in Ukraine before World War II. For the Armenians, the mountainous region of Karabakh had always possessed a degree of autonomy, even under Persian rule. The primordialist discourse of the de facto states strengthens their claims to absolute sovereignty: any compromise of their independence would be a violation of the very trends of history.

As well as claiming historical legitimacy, the de facto states also see themselves as morally entitled to statehood. For instance, according to Sergei Shamba, "We have a right to self-determination because of the Georgian acts of genocide and aggression conducted against Abkhazia."[21] Similarly, Grigory Maracutsa argued, "Pridnestrovye is a sovereign and independent state because the Republic of Moldova attempted to resolve the conflict through the use of force. Seven hundred were killed and three thousand wounded from this act of aggression."[22] The Armenians of Karabakh interpret Azerbaijani attempts to restore control through the prism of their devastating experience within the Ottoman Empire in 1915. All the separatist authorities insist on an inherent moral entitlement to self-determination when faced with "alien" and "imposed" rule. In so doing, they acknowledge that the rules allowing for self-determination are now limited. However, leaders in every de facto state argue that international law is an organic and flexible process. In their view, the current rules were designed for the era of decolonization, and they have faith that this regime will change eventually in their favor. In the words of the legal adviser to the Armenian foreign minister, "recognition always follows events, as does the international community."[23]

The de facto states will wait until the application of the right to self-determination widens. Border changes and the creation of new states were part and parcel of European affairs prior to the twentieth century. In the view of the de facto state authorities, there is no reason that this flexibility will not return to international relations.

The insistence on sovereignty by the de facto states has several effects. First, it means that conflict settlement may not be reached through federalizing power-sharing arrangements. It is often assumed in Chisinau, Tbilisi, and Baku, as well as in European capitals, that the "statehood" of these entities is a resource that they will be willing to bargain away once the circumstances are propitious. Many peace proposals put forward over the past decade have been based on notions of federal power sharing between the metropolitan and de facto states. The assumption underlying these proposals is that sovereignty is the maximal—and thus, by definition, *negotiable*—aim of these breakaway areas, and that their minimal and nonnegotiable objective resides at some lower form of autonomy. In fact, sovereignty is entirely nonnegotiable in their eyes. The separatist state authorities may be willing to negotiate a new relationship with the metropolitan states, but not one based on a federation. The exact appellation of the new state that will emerge from this new relationship is also negotiable. However, at the most, the self-declared states may accept confederal ties with the metropolitan state.

A confederation has elements of power sharing, but they do not infringe on the internal sovereignty of its constituent subjects. All the de facto states insist on developing voluntary and equal ties with their former rulers. In their view, cooperation could be extensive in certain areas, such as trade, customs, and communications, but it would not infringe on their basic sovereignty. In the negotiations that have occurred in all of these conflicts, the separatist areas have supported the proposals put forward for "common statehood" with the metropolitan state, which draw on confederal thinking. Moldova and the PMR reached an agreement in 1997 to create a common state within the borders of Moldova.[24] In the view of the PMR, it would take the form of a voluntary union of two equal states under a common and shared framework. According to Valery Litskai, the PMR foreign minister, the common state is the solution by which the PMR can square the circle of maintaining its sovereignty and independence intact while integrating into the international community and world affairs.[25] To return to the words of Vladimir Bodnar, the head of the PMR Security Committee, the de facto states are willing to remain "islands" surrounded by states as long as they maintain supreme control over their territory and people.

Moldova, Georgia, and Azerbaijan have rejected confederal proposals as threats to their own sovereignty. A confederal structure might indeed enshrine the right of its constituent parts to withdraw from the common state. These governments fear that the separatist authorities would secede legally as soon as they could justify doing so.[26] Moreover, the metropolitan capitals are reluctant to abandon one of their strongest weapons with regard to their separatist regions: withholding formal recognition of their existence. This weapon keeps the self-declared states in pariah status in international relations. It also ensures that the metropolitan state can consider using all means at its disposal, including force, to restore its territorial integrity at some point in the future, in the meantime keeping the situation tense in and around the de facto states.

The second effect stemming from the insistence on absolute sovereignty concerns internally displaced persons and refugees in the conflicts in Abkhazia and Nagorno-Karabakh. The de facto states' insistence on internal sovereignty means in practice that they are unwilling to welcome back the IDPs who fled during the wars. Demography resides at the heart of the conflicts. Before the war, the Georgians were a plurality of inhabitants of the Abkhaz region. According to the census of 1989, the total population was 525,000, of whom more than 95,000 were Abkhaz, while the Georgians numbered over 230,000. The Georgian population lived in a compact majority in the Gali region while the Abkhaz held a majority in Gudauta, but the rest of Abkhazia had intermingled populations. In the capital, Sukhumi, for example, the

Georgian share of the population stood at 42 percent, Russians accounted for 22 percent, and Abkhaz made up 13 percent.

Abkhazia's Georgian population fled as an indirect consequence of the war of 1992–94. They were also one of the war's targets. The Abkhaz authorities feared the extinction of Abkhaz culture and language and eventually of the Abkhaz people—a fate similar to that which had befallen other numerically modest peoples in the Caucasus. Abkhaz self-determination has been founded on the absence of the Georgian population from the historically claimed Abkhaz land. In the separatist view, "citizenship" of the self-declared Abkhaz state cannot be allowed to include the displaced Georgian population, as this would leave the Abkhaz as a small minority once again. In the Abkhaz view, the very idea behind the new Abkhaz state would not survive such a threat.

Demographics have placed Abkhazia in an extremely uncomfortable position. Its authorities argue that Abkhaz is not a nation-state built for the Abkhaz alone, but a multinational state that includes important Armenian and Russian minorities. However, ethnic Abkhaz hold most of the important positions in the self-declared state. In 1989, Armenians and Russians together accounted for 28.9 percent of the population of the region (14.6 percent and 14.3 percent, respectively); that is, they outnumbered the ethnic Abkhaz. Since the war the numbers of Armenians and Russians have dwindled, with the Russian population falling particularly sharply. Albert Topalyan, head of the Armenian Krunk Association, estimated in 2000 that the Armenian population had been reduced by 30 percent.[27] Even so, in Topalyan's view, the Abkhaz still now accounted for barely half of the population of their self-declared state, their numbers standing at about 90,000, while the Armenians numbered about 50,000 and, together with the Russians, made up a large part of the population. In the words of one member of the political opposition in Abkhazia: "The Abkhaz state treats the non-Abkhaz quite badly. There is no discrimination, but there is no support to Armenian or

Russian schools for example. The Armenians and the Russians are the most vulnerable of all."[28] In addition, the Abkhaz state faces another dilemma in Gali, where large numbers of ethnic Georgians (estimated at around 40,000) have returned unofficially to their former homes inside Abkhazia to farm its rich land.

The tight link between ethnicity and land in these conflicts makes the return of refugees and IDPs difficult to consider for the de facto state. For practical reasons (it does not really control the area) and under pressure from the international community, the Abkhaz government has allowed tens of thousands of Georgians to return to the Gali region. This Georgian population has become a source of predatory "taxation" by various Abkhaz (and Georgian) forces. However, the Abkhaz government will not formally recognize this return or register this population for voting in Abkhaz elections from fear of the Abkhaz becoming a minority in their own land once again.

The case of Nagorno-Karabakh is different. Over 80 percent of the Azerbaijani IDPs lived in the seven districts of Azerbaijani territory that are occupied by Karabakh forces but that are not inside Nagorno-Karabakh itself. These lands were occupied in 1993 and 1994 to create a security buffer for the self-declared state and as bargaining chips in the peace process. The separatists could countenance easily the return of Azerbaijani IDPs to at least six of these districts (Lachin is questionable for the Karabakh authorities as it remains the main link to Armenia). However, the repatriation of the Azerbaijani population to towns and areas inside Karabakh itself, such as the town of Shusha, which towers above Stepanakert, would be more difficult for the separatist authorities to accept.

Fear and Insecurity

Insecurity represents another internal force driving the de facto states. Behind all the rhetoric of sovereignty, self-determination, and justice are calculations of power that have led the separatist authorities to seek security based on force.

Fear was one factor that gave rise to the conflicts at their outset. In late March 1992, the first Moldovan president, Mircea Snegur, declared a state of emergency that set the two parties on the path toward greater clashes than those that had occurred already. In early April, the Moldovan government tried and failed to regain by force control of the town of Bendery. It again sent troops to Bendery on June 19. Armed clashes followed and the PMR fledgling forces were able to repulse the Moldovan attempt only with armored support from the Russian 14th Army deployed on the left bank of the Dnestr River (then under the command of Aleksandr Lebed). Moldova and the PMR fought not a war but rather a series of limited armed clashes and incurred close to a thousand casualties. This number pales in comparison to losses in the Yugoslav wars and the conflicts in the Caucasus, but it is significant in terms of its impact on the local population in an urban context. In any case, the conflict was seized upon by the authorities of the PMR as justification for their independence. The new Moldova was seen to be a Romanianizing state, in which the traditionally more Slavic and more russophone elites on the left bank would be sidelined. The armed clashes confirmed the threat posed by the new authorities in Chisinau to the political and economic power held by the left-bank elites.

Fear was also a driving force behind the conflicts in Georgia and Azerbaijan. In 1991, the first Georgian president, Zviad Gamsakhurdia, unilaterally abolished South Ossetia's status of autonomy in Georgia, and armed clashes between Georgian and South Ossetian militias spread throughout the region. In August 1992, Georgian guardsmen seized Sukhumi by force. In the eyes of the tiny Abkhaz and Ossetian minorities, the new Georgian state seemed bent on asserting by force its power over all of Georgia. The unifying idea (which quickly became disunifying) then driving the new Republic of Georgia was preponderant power in Georgian hands in Tbilisi. For the Abkhaz, their very existence as a people and culture was seen to be at stake. Similarly, in Nagorno-Karabakh the Armenian population lived in a vulnerable enclave in Azerbaijan, surrounded by perceived potential enemies. The Armenian authorities in Stepanakert and Yerevan feared a new twist in a regionwide history of Armenian defeat.

Insecurity has remained a defining condition of life since the end of the wars in each de facto state. The cease-fires reached in Moldova (1992), Georgia (South Ossetia in 1992 and Abkhazia in 1994), and Azerbaijan (1994) reflect victories the separatists reached on the battlefield. Historically, these peoples have rarely, if ever, won wars by themselves and for themselves. Victory has left the de facto states bewildered. And fearful.

On the one hand, victory is a source of strength. Natella Akaba, leader of the Center for Human Rights and Support for Democracy in Abkhazia, argued that the Abkhaz victory was "a fundamental basis of legitimacy" for the self-declared state.[29] The victories of the early 1990s have become sacred objects that may not be questioned. Naira Melkoumian, the Nagorno-Karabakh foreign minister, stated, "After a history of tragedy, we have won a war at last!"[30] The authorities are determined at all costs to retain the fruits of victory. As during the armed phases of the conflicts, the security strategies of the de facto states remain total. In the separatists' view, the threat posed by the metropolitan states is seen as existential and itself total. Melkoumian argued, "History gave Armenia so little territory. We cannot make any concessions that would threaten Armenia and Nagorno-Karabakh."[31] In addition, compromise would raise questions about the nature of the sacrifice suffered by many during and since the conflicts. As time passes since actual fighting, the significance of victory takes on new connotations. Facing times of isolation and penury, lives that may otherwise seem bleak gain some meaning from victory.

On the other hand, the separatist authorities profoundly distrust victory. They are all aware that they have won a battle and not the war. The example of renewed war in Chechnya has been instructive in this respect. The Speaker of the Abkhaz parliament,

Sokrat Jinjolian, was blunt about the situation with Georgia: "The resumption of war is a real possibility."[32] An Abkhaz civil society activist also put it bluntly: "Many Abkhaz have stopped trusting peace. Peace is a deceit; peace is a time when the enemy gathers strength, a breathing space."[33] The sense of threat posed by the metropolitan state is perceived as real in the de facto state, even if the metropolitan state's armed forces are weak and unlikely to be able to use force on the scale employed by Russia in Chechnya since 1999. The distrust of victory has led the de facto states to elevate self-defense over all other policy areas. None of the de facto states are military-ruled states; all of them, however, are devoted to the military.

War and the necessity of war making were formative features of the state-making process in modern Europe. These forces play a similar formative role in the post-Soviet self-declared states. In essence, during the war in Nagorno-Karabakh and Abkhazia, the armed forces *were* the state, without which the self-determination movements would have ceased to exist as political forces. Since the cease-fires, these states have moved to create genuine military structures. As the state of war is seen to still exist, the armed forces are designed to ensure security through deterring the metropolitan state. The Abkhaz armed forces stand at around two thousand strong, with a mobilization capacity of perhaps four times this number, and they are equipped with very small numbers of battle tanks, armored personnel carriers, and artillery and a few converted naval vessels. Their organization and training follow a classic Soviet cadre/reserve force approach, founded on the notion of rapid mobilization and a heavily armed population.[34] South Ossetia maintains one motor-rifle battalion, made up of fifteen hundred troops. The PMR has armed forces totaling about five thousand, including various other security forces, interior troops, and customs and border forces, as well as a Cossack battalion. Nagorno-Karabakh is very different, as its armed forces are integrated into Armenian military structures and

number around fifteen thousand troops, with a powerful equipment and weapons base.

These states vary in their ability to maintain deterrence. The
line of contact between Azerbaijani and Armenian forces is a
well-defined trench system, which experiences only occasional
violations of the cease-fire regime. In contrast, in the border district of Gali inside Abkhazia, Georgian paramilitary groups are
active in rendering the area lawless. The Abkhaz, especially, mis-
trust their victory. In the view of the separatist authorities, the
war is continuing by other means, via the trade restrictions, the
activities of the Georgian paramilitary groups, and Georgian
preparations for new war. As the Abkhaz defense minister stated:
"The whole world helps the Georgian armed forces. . . . Who is
Georgia preparing to fight? Against Russia? No. Against Turkey?
No. They are preparing to fight Abkhazia. All of the preparations
are designed against Abkhazia."[35]

The construction of military systems is part of the separatists'
state-building projects. Universal male conscription is in force
in all the self-declared states and provides a reserve base in case
of renewed conflict. It also performs an important socialization
function in giving groups of young men some understanding,
however limited and fragile, of the new state and its significance
and history. In these states, which face immediate external threats,
the values of discipline, order, and valor are seen as vitally important to develop in the young male population. The effectiveness
of that socialization function is difficult to assess. Certainly, the
extreme conditions of service tend to undermine its success. However, the need to serve and acquire training seems to be recognized by most young men in these areas. Also, for the very limited numbers of conscientious objectors, there are alternative
service programs. In Nagorno-Karabakh, university-educated students are sent out to front-line areas to teach a range of subjects
at all levels in makeshift schools.[36]

Fear and insecurity are also instruments of the separatist authorities in their state-building projects, although these projects

are as weak as the states themselves. Since the early 1990s, the metropolitan states have started to move away from exclusive and antagonistic state-building projects, and more moderate politicians have led the movement toward state consolidation. (This is not to say that radical political groups no longer exist in each of the metropolitan states. The extremist rhetoric of the early 1990s regarding the separatist regions can still be heard.) In contrast, the political tenor in the de facto states has shifted very little during this time. Public rhetoric has remained largely defined by dichotomies of "us versus them." The threatening existence of the "other"—the former central authorities—is used to justify the very existence of the de facto state. The existential challenge posed by the former central power is a powerful glue binding the residual populations of these areas together. It is part of the "idea" that builds popular support for the de facto states. The discourse of insecurity makes reconciliation and notions of power sharing very difficult to accept, as it has primordialized and totalized the conflicts with the metropolitan states.[37] In the PMR, Chisinau is referred to as a "national socialist clique."[38] Potential compromise has become all the more difficult to justify, especially as new generations of Abkhaz, Ossets, and Karabakhstis are born who have never lived with Georgian or Azeri neighbors and have been brought up on a story of metropolitan state aggression.

Three conclusions flow from the condition and exploitation of insecurity. First, de facto states are racketeer states. As defined by Charles Tilly in his discussion of the birth of states in Europe, "someone who produces the danger and, at a price, the shield against it is a racketeer."[39] This point is not theoretical but a factor built into the very structure of the de facto states that further supports their survival and entrenches the status quo. While the metropolitan states indeed pose a real threat to the de facto states, the emphasis placed on the metropolitan threat goes beyond a rational assessment of what the de facto states need to respond to this threat.

The PMR is a case in point. Any objective assessment of the threat posed by Moldova to the PMR would conclude that it is almost nil—in terms of both the capabilities of the Moldovan armed forces, which are very weak, and the intentions of most of the political elite in Chisinau, who do not envisage a forceful solution to the conflict. However, the PMR Ministry of Security—led by a former Soviet special forces officer wanted by Interpol for crimes committed in the Baltic states, Vladimir Antiufeev (an alias)—runs a number of social organizations and newspapers that inflate the nature of the Moldovan threat to Transnistria. The Ministry of Security conflates this imaginary Moldovan threat with the intentions of the so-called aggressive Western alliance and the "revanchist fascist" regime in Romania.[40] The sense of threat thus engendered serves to justify the extensive role played by the Security Ministry in all aspects of political and economic life in the PMR. The motto of the Ministry of Security newspaper, *Molodezhnyi Marzh*, is, indeed, "We Always Know More."

This logic affects more than just the Ministry of Security—the existence of the PMR itself depends on the supposed threat posed by Moldova and the West. An existential threat that hardly exists has become a fundamental pillar justifying the existence of the de facto state—in essence, this is racketeering.

The racketeering dimension also affects civil-military relations in these states. In Nagorno-Karabakh, the racketeering tendency made the former defense minister, Samvel Babayan, the most powerful economic and political actor until March 2000, when he was arrested for the attempted assassination of the Nagorno-Karabakh president. The president and government have sought since to reduce the political influence of the military. In an interview in August 2000, Prime Minister Anushavan Danielyan stated: "The armed forces should not be distinct or separated from the government—not a force of its own. . . . All must obey the law. . . . The armed forces hold the line. That is all."[41] The Nagorno-Karabakh foreign minister, Naira Melkoumian, argued further that the overwhelming power held by the military had undermined popular faith in the authorities.[42] "In war," she continued, "the military is by necessity critical in decision-making. But now, people will not put up with this situation. . . . The military must work on military affairs and civilians must work in the civilian world."[43] The situation was similar in South Ossetia, where until 2003 the Tedeyev brothers had a lock on the security forces, giving them access to illicit economic resources and automatic political power.

The existence of an external threat, and its instrumental use, has distorted civil-military relations in the self-declared states. At the very least, as in Abkhazia and the PMR, the military and security agencies dominate security policy making. At the most, as in Nagorno-Karabakh, the military dominates politics. The inflated role of the military represents an important obstacle to conflict settlement as the logic of military dominance has become deeply entrenched.

The second conclusion prompted by the nature and manipulation of insecurity is that self-declared states have no faith in the rule of law as a means to guarantee their security. Military power is seen as the only way to deter the metropolitan states from seeking to resolve the conflicts by force. The distrust of law is partly a legacy of the Soviet Union, where politics were founded on rule *by* law and not *of* law. Also, in the early 1990s, the separatist regions experienced how new laws (constitutions, declarations, resolutions, and so forth) enacted in the metropolitan capitals were used as weapons against them. As noted by Svante Cornell, "there is no confidence in the implementation of the basic principle of international law, *pacta sund servanda* [agreements must be kept]."[44]

This distrust has implications for the nature of any agreed-on future relationship between the de facto and metropolitan states. In particular, it is difficult to imagine that the self-declared authorities will agree to federation-type relations, where, by definition, ties between federal subjects and the federal center are based on the transformation of fundamental political questions into legal questions.[45] Any settlement of these conflicts must consider at its heart the requirements of deterrence and security if the de facto state is to be willing to compromise on the victories achieved on the battlefield.

The third conclusion regarding insecurity concerns the ability of the international community to provide the necessary hard guarantees required by the de facto states before they accept a settlement. In the former Soviet Union, peacekeeping operations have been largely discredited as impartial mechanisms to support a mediated peace process.[46] As discussed below, the Russian use of peacekeeping as a means to promote its interests played an important role in this. The PMR and Abkhazia view Russian operations as a key security guarantee against renewed encroachment by the metropolitan states. As a result, they have been unwilling to change the mandates of these operations or to replace Russian with international forces, as has been requested by the metropolitan states. For Bodnar, the chairman of the PMR parliamentary security committee, "this is one of the best peacekeeping models in the world: The parties are compelled to become peacekeepers!"[47] The Abkhaz foreign minister made the point more bluntly: "The CIS peacekeeping forces have de facto established a state border."[48]

In contrast, the far more powerfully armed Nagorno-Karabakh has been unwilling to place its security in the hands of a peacekeeping operation—especially if the operation is international and the peacekeepers unarmed. As noted by Foreign Minister Melkoumian, "if we find a mutually acceptable solution, there will be no need for international troops. We have held the cease-fire for seven years without any problems."[49] A settlement of the conflict in Nagorno-Karabakh, therefore, will have to address the Karabakh Armenian insistence that their own military power be the primary security guarantee against any future conflict. In the former Soviet Union, peacekeeping operations are not obvious solutions to these conflicts. In Moldova and Georgia, these operations have in fact become part of the problem.

Subsistence Syndromes

The de facto states are failing states. They may have the institutional fixtures of statehood, but they cannot provide for its substance. The wars of the early 1990s devastated their economies and exacerbated the difficulties that resulted from the collapse of the Soviet economic system. Since the cease-fires, little progress has occurred toward economic reform. The enduring threat of war has combined with economic mismanagement to produce hyperinflation, de-monetized economies, the collapse of social services, and the extensive criminalization of economic activities. These problems have been exacerbated by the legal limbo in which all of these de facto states exist, as nonrecognized strips of no-man's-land.

In the cases of Abkhazia and Nagorno-Karabakh, economic trade restrictions have become the main tools wielded by the metropolitan state against the separatists. Abkhazia has lived under a CIS-wide sanctions regime since January 1996. Azerbaijan and Turkey imposed economic blockades on Nagorno-Karabakh and Armenia early in the war. The economic tool as used by Azerbaijan and Georgia has two aims: first, to compel the separatist areas to compromise in the negotiations; and second, to ensure that the de facto state does not prosper while the negotiations are under way. The economic tool has also been praised as potentially positive by the international community, which hopes that the de facto states will be encouraged to compromise by the promise of eventual assistance for reconstruction and reform.

On both accounts, the economic tool plays a far less important role than is assumed. The positive attraction of potential international assistance is attenuated by the fact that the de facto states are driven first and foremost by political, not economic, imperatives. They are political animals. The Nagorno-Karabakh prime minister admitted to me that the main problem he faced was the need to rebuild the economy: "But independence is more important than the economy, and this will not be exchanged for anything. Freedom stands above all other questions."[50] The severe economic difficulties of these states have not compelled them to compromise. On the contrary, economic isolation has only strengthened subsistence syndromes in which the authorities are determined to survive at all costs and have developed structures that are appropriate for this purpose. The subsistence syndromes, which are based on a combination of firm political determination, deep economic weakness, and extensive criminalization, are a key part of the internal logic sustaining the de facto states.[51]

All of these states have dwindling and aging populations. Many of those who could do so have fled, mainly to Russia. Significant proportions of the remaining populations are made up of the weak and the vulnerable and those who have nowhere else to go. As already noted, the situation is dramatic in the PMR, where the ratio of workers to pensioners is said to be 1.5:1, an economically unsustainable situation. Similarly, the Abkhaz government cannot meet the needs of its pensioners, who have been left to fend for themselves with limited support from international nongovernmental organizations.

The people of the de facto states put up with desperate conditions for three reasons. First, many cannot leave and thus have no choice. Second, the economies of the states from which they separated are almost as bad as theirs—and, what is more relevant, the population and authorities in the separatist states *perceive* the economic situation to be worse in the metropolitan states. In economic terms, therefore, there would appear to be little incentive for them to reintegrate with their former ruler. Third, and most crucially, the security imperative is seen as far more important than the economic imperative by the separatist authorities and their populations.

The residual populations in all of the de facto states have become deeply impoverished. However, it is no accident that the separatist states are not near the Arctic Circle—sunny and favorable climates, beneficial geographical positions with access to the

Black Sea and important rivers, and fertile lands are key to their continuing survival. People have retreated into difficult but sustainable subsistence strategies.[52]

Despite the support of Yerevan and extensive Armenian diaspora assistance, Nagorno-Karabakh suffers from agricultural and industrial collapse. Small-scale workshops have been built, but these are hardly numerous enough to employ the working population. Clutching at straws, in 2000 the government hailed as a success the creation of 560 jobs. According to the Karabakh minister for economics and reconstruction, less than 10 percent of the industrial potential of Nagorno-Karabakh is being used relative to the 1980s.[53] The privatization of Karabakh agriculture has thrown the system back to subsistence farming, with very few inputs, little use of machinery, and very low production levels. As a result, conditions in Karabakh villages have become desperate. In the words of the mayor of the village of Karintak, "people are so poor, and they have no way of exiting this poverty because there are absolutely no jobs."[54] In this showcase village, according to the mayor, there are 617 adults, of whom 230 are unemployed officially. Unofficially, however, almost all of them are unemployed.

Before the war, the economy of the Abkhaz region was dependent on tourism and the export of subtropical produce such as tea, tobacco, and citrus fruits. Since then, in the words of the economics minister, "all of the main bases of the economy—we have lost!"[55] Georgian forces occupied much of Abkhaz territory for over a year, and marauding and looting were extensive. Since 1996, the CIS sanctions have deprived Abkhazia of its main sources of revenue. On the whole, the region has retreated to subsistence farming and dependency on international nongovernmental support. The former state farms and tea plantations are largely overgrown, with large tracts of arable land left idle. Most men are unemployed. With the renewal of war in Chechnya, the Russian government closed the Russian-Abkhaz border to men between the ages 10 and 65. As a result, Abkhaz women had to shuttle back and forth across the border, bringing in most of the goods sold in the markets of Abkhazia's capital.

The PMR state survives on the revenue garnered from one or two industrial plants that have been modernized and still work. The Moldova Steel Works in Rybnitsa, which employs close to four thousand workers, is the source of 40 to 50 percent of the de facto state's revenue. A minority of the working population is involved in all sorts of trading activities, many illegal, which take advantage of the benefits of the PMR's geographical position, sandwiched between Ukraine and Romania and close to the key Black Sea port of Odessa. But the great majority of the PMR population lives in deep poverty, with an average income of one U.S. dollar a day. The government is deeply indebted to Russia for energy resources and faces pressure to increase prices of gas and oil to repay the debts—yet the government also fears that price hikes may provoke social unrest.

Inside the de facto states, political stability is founded on corrupt corporatism. The authorities have sought to neutralize potential threats by co-opting them. In these economies, shadowy figures often play government-supported monopolistic roles. In the PMR, the financial-industrial group Sheriff is owned by a former member of the police who runs important sectors of the separatist economy, including several cable television stations, the only telephone communications company in the region (Inter-DnestrCom—which follows the U.S. CDMA standard, whereas Moldova adheres to the European GSM standard), the weekly newspaper *Delo*, a Western-standard supermarket chain, and a series of gasoline stations throughout Transnistria. The Sheriff Group has interests in all profitable services that have developed in the breakaway state, which it played a key role in developing in the first place. In exchange, the Sheriff Group performs social functions for the state, including the construction of a new cathedral called Christ's Rebirth and a religious school in the head city of Tiraspol.

Other key parts of the PMR population have also been given special privileges, such as tax cuts and protected legal status. For example, the Black Sea Cossacks are legally considered a not-for-profit charity in the PMR, which leaves all their activities as traders and service providers tax-exempt. In exchange, the Cossacks represent a source of support to President Smirnov (himself an honorary Cossack colonel). They also perform a range of social services; for example, the Black Sea Cossacks built a park in Tiraspol in 2000 dedicated to the veterans of World War II. The mingling of crime and state structures is dramatic in the PMR, where a ruthless form of state-private capitalism has been created while statues of Lenin remain standing in the streets and parks. During his visit to the PMR in April 2001, Boris Pastukhov, deputy chairman (under Yevgeny Primakov) of the Russian Special Committee for Negotiations on the PMR created by Vladimir Putin in 2000, described the PMR bluntly: "[Russia] shall no longer tolerate the foolishness, boorishness, and thievishness of some Dnestr politicians. . . . We have understood that there are some people in the Dnestr region who are parasitic on warfare and political chaos, as each day brings more fortunes to them—they are kings in their own kingdom, where neither law nor common sense works."[56]

The armed forces are very well protected in the separatist states. In Nagorno-Karabakh, the military became the most prominent political-economic actor under former defense minister Samvel Babayan. Babayan was able to benefit from his position to secure a monopoly over the cigarette and gasoline trade in the republic, and he also operated the Jupiter company in a family member's name. Babayan's control over military procurement put him in a golden position to profit from the construction of the Karabakh armed forces after the 1994 cease-fire. The Tedeyev brothers operated a similar racket in South Ossetia. In Abkhazia, trade in timber and sales of protected hardwood are run through the state-owned AbkhazLes, which is tied to the family

of President Vladislav Ardzinba. Private Turkish ships frequently
run the CIS blockade to buy Abkhaz timber at Sukhumi.

Groups inside and outside the de facto states profit from
the status quo. Crime and illegal economic activities have come to
reside at the heart of these conflicts. Charles King links this crime
to the weakness of the metropolitan states: "State weakness is of
obvious benefit to the unrecognized regimes. Business can be
carried on without paying production taxes or tariffs."[57] These
activities include large-scale cigarette and alcohol smuggling from
the PMR to Moldova to avoid the payment of sales taxes. According to Bushulyak, a member of the Moldovan Expert Group for
negotiations with the PMR in 2000, such smuggling has become a
"major, major problem" for Moldova, with millions of dollars lost
in state revenue.[58] "The entire eastern front is open," he said.
Clearly, important forces in Moldova profit from this situation.

For example, the PMR steelworks at Rybnitsa, which is one of
the mainstays of PMR independence, is not a full-cycle factory.
Moldova provides 50 percent of the scrap metals for it. Most
important, this strategically important factory exported steel to
world markets, mainly the United States, with Moldovan customs
stamps, initially provided to the PMR by Chisinau in February
1996. A number of figures in the Moldovan government profited
greatly from this very lucrative trade. Russian groups have also invested in the PMR. Most notably, the Russian-owned gas provider
Itera, which is based offshore but has close ties to the Russian
gas giant Gazprom, is the majority owner of the Rybnitsa steelworks, having invested an estimated U.S.$100 million in the plant
since 1998. Similarly, South Ossetia has become a major channel
for smuggled goods to and from Georgia and Russia—including
most of the flour and grain sold in Georgia.

Crime mingles with geopolitics in these conflicts in an un-
settling manner. Since their deployment, Russian peacekeeping
troops have become involved in smuggling activities across the
front lines in Georgia and Moldova. In the Gali region of Abkhazia, crime and smuggling have become dominant ways of life

for the vulnerable Georgians who have returned, the Georgian paramilitary groups that are active there, and the Russian peace-keeping troops. The trade in hazelnuts and citrus fruits, and also gasoline from the Russian Federation, has blurred the lines between ethnic groups in the conflict, uniting them all in the search for profit.

It is clear that enough people, inside and outside the de facto states, profit enough from the states' existence to make the status quo durable. A perverted and weak, but workable, incentive structure has emerged over the past decade that sustains the separatist areas.

EXTERNAL DRIVERS

These internal forces combine with three categories of external forces to sustain the de facto states: the roles played by the metropolitan states; Russian intervention; and the support, both formal and informal, of other states and organizations.

The Role of the Metropolitan States

Moldova, Georgia, and Azerbaijan themselves play important roles in sustaining the status quo. This is not to blame these states for the impasse, but it is important to recognize their part more clearly. The role of the metropolitan states is both indirect and direct.

At the *indirect* level, Moldova, Georgia, and Azerbaijan cannot entice the separatist areas into restoring either political or economic relations with them. As already mentioned, the authorities of the de facto states believe that their own economic predicament is no worse, and perhaps even better, than the economic situation facing the metropolitan states. While admitting the difficulties caused by not having access to international financial institutions, the PMR authorities noted to me on several occasions, not without a hint of glee, that the PMR does not have external debts, as does Moldova. In February 2001, the Union of

PMR Moldovans (still the ethnic majority in the breakaway state) issued a statement that described Moldova as a country "on the verge of complete catastrophe, ruled by the IMF and leading Western nations." In 1996–97, when the Georgian GDP was growing at almost 10 percent annually, the Abkhaz authorities may have looked across the Inguri River with some envy. However, the collapse of the Georgian economy since 1998, following the Russian ruble crisis, and the increasing evidence of endemic corruption have reinforced the Abkhaz perspective of the limited prospects for economic cooperation with Tbilisi. Similarly, the Karabakh authorities are worried about the oil dividends that Azerbaijan will secure over the next decade but are also increasingly aware of the decreasing importance of Caspian Sea oil on the international market.

More fundamentally, the nature of politics in the former centers has reinforced the de facto states' determination to resist reconciliation with the metropolitan states. Radical nationalist parties continue to exist in all the metropolitan states, allowing the separatist authorities to justify the possibility of renewed war. In Georgia, for example, the Temporary Committee for Abkhazeti was created in January 2000 and pledged to liberate the region by the spring of that year. In addition, since the early 1990s, the Georgian government has subsidized structures of government for Abkhazia in exile. Tbilisi provides support to the Executive Council of the Autonomous Republic of Abkhazia, which has twenty-five delegates and a supreme presidium. The ethnically Georgian government in exile maintains eleven ministries, thirteen state committees, nine general offices, and five inspectorates. There has also been an Abkhaz faction in the Georgian parliament, made up of Georgian former members of the Abkhaz parliament from before the war. The Deputy Speaker of the Georgian parliament before the "Rose Revolution" of November 2003 was a member of this faction.

This ponderous and expensive government in exile performs an important service for the Georgian government in channeling the political force of the quarter-million-strong IDP population into state-led mechanisms. (Two assassination attempts on Eduard Shevardnadze while he was president have made the Georgian authorities very conscious of the dangers of uncontrolled political disaffection.) Government support of these structures acts as a control valve in domestic politics. However, this support does nothing to increase the confidence of the separatist Abkhaz authorities that Tbilisi is genuinely interested in their view. The existence of Abkhazia-in-exile reinforces the separatists' view that Tbilisi has not recognized their position as having any legitimacy and still sees them as a fifth column for the return of the Russian empire. In addition, the activities of the Georgian "partisan" groups strengthen Abkhaz contentions that Tbilisi seeks to undermine Sukhumi by force. It is an open secret that the "partisans" receive unofficial support from the Georgian government, including advanced weaponry, remote-controlled mines, and night-vision equipment. Periodic statements by Shevardnadze about the possible use of force in Abkhazia also did nothing to reassure Sukhumi.

The protection of human and national minority rights has remained problematic in the metropolitan states. In Azerbaijan, in particular, the treatment of national minorities and ordinary citizens has been blemished by strong-arm tactics of the police and security forces, which have been noted publicly by international human rights organizations. In the Georgian case, a prominent member of Abkhaz civil society stated: "Abkhaz society is not convinced that Georgia is a democratic state. In the absence of a conciliatory tone in Georgia and with no sense of culpability for instigating the war, Abkhazia believes that Georgia is an unreliable partner with which to build a common state."

At the indirect level, therefore, not enough change has occurred in the politics and economics of the metropolitan states to convince the separatist authorities to seek renewed ties through compromise. The words of Paata Zakareishvili, a moderate Georgian political commentator, are striking: "What has

Georgia done to make Georgia more attractive to Abkhazia? Georgia is hardly attractive to Georgians."[59]

Moldova, Georgia, and Azerbaijan also play a *direct* role in feeding the status quo. A first direct dimension centers on the question of economic ties between the metropolitan and separatist areas. On this point, the metropolitan states face a real dilemma. One option for them is to develop economic ties with the separatist area, as Moldova has done officially since 1996 and informally since the day fighting stopped in July 1992. While certain groups in Moldova have profited from this cooperation, it has done nothing to decrease the number of PMR customs and border posts illegally deployed in the security zone along the Dnestr River. Nor has it increased the degree of trust between the two parties—on the contrary, this cooperation has only been exploited by the separatist authorities to boost their profits and strengthen their independence.

The other option available for the metropolitan states is to blockade the separatist areas, an option pursued by Georgia and Azerbaijan. The blockades have deeply affected the economic development of the separatist states; however, every official and academic analysis of these blockades has highlighted their counterproductive effect. They have served only to entrench the intractability of the de facto authorities and pushed them to develop skewed, but workable, subsistence economies. Moreover, the blockades are used by the separatist authorities to justify the weakness of their economies, with all of their own failings explained away as the consequences of the aggressive policies of the enemy. The blockades have become "get-out-of-jail-free cards" for the separatist leaders. In terms of economic policies, therefore, both paths followed by the metropolitan states have worked to strengthen the logic sustaining the de facto states.

Moreover, the existence of de facto states inside the metropolitan borders is not entirely undesirable for the central governments—the situation would be worse for Chisinau, Tbilisi, and Baku should the international community recognize the de facto states. The existence of nonrecognized areas means that the metropolitan states are not compelled to recognize the defeat they suffered in the wars of the early 1990s. "Georgia refuses to draw the obvious conclusion from its defeat in Abkhazia," Paata Zakareishvili has argued. "Instead it prefers to wallow in its injured pride and wait for someone else to solve its problems."[60] It is safe and easy to wallow. The open recognition of defeat and the loss of historical homelands would challenge political stability and threaten the current leadership and their successors. Particularly in Georgia and Azerbaijan, strong opposition forces exist that would readily seize such an opportunity to attack any government of compromise as "defeatist."

Moldova, Georgia, and Azerbaijan are fragile, newly independent states with weak political institutions and very limited resources that have embarked on a difficult process of nation and state building. As respected Georgian commentator David Darchiashvili told me in an interview on August 6, 2000, "the new Georgia would not survive the open loss of Abkhazia—it would not withstand the shock." The reality is that Georgia has already lost Abkhazia. Nonrecognition of the separatist state allows Georgia to continue living a dream of national and territorial unity. Put bluntly, the status quo allows the metropolitan authorities to avoid grasping the nettle of defeat.

In the case of Georgia, the limbo status of Abkhazia also has allowed Tbilisi to use means of coercion short of war to undermine the separatist regime. The tools included the sanctions regime and support to the Georgian paramilitary groups engaged in subversive activities. Moreover, the status quo allows Moldova, Georgia, and Azerbaijan to focus on domestic areas that are perceived to be more vital for their future: attracting foreign direct investment, developing strategic areas of their economies, and pursuing economic reform. In the case of Azerbaijan, the governments under Heydar Aliyev adopted a "wait-and-strengthen" policy after the war, based on the promise of massive profits from the development of Azerbaijan's energy reserves. Heydar's son and successor as president, Ilham, seems unlikely to change this policy.

The metropolitan states accepted the cease-fires in the early 1990s to gain time, which all of them saw as playing in their favor. The status quo is seen as a window of opportunity in which to gain external sources of support and strengthen the metropolitan state, while the separatist area is blockaded and undermined.

The Russian Role

As the former imperial center, Russia plays a fundamental role in these conflicts. Russian intervention was important in the outbreak of the conflicts in Moldova and Georgia, and Russian peacekeeping forces are now deployed on what have become de facto borders with the separatist regions in these two states. Russia has also been deeply involved in the Karabakh conflict in both military and political terms. Since the end of the wars, which the separatist forces won partly with Russian assistance, Russian policy toward these conflicts has retained enough ambiguity to reinforce the status quo and protect the de facto states. Russian engagement operates on several levels, illustrating the multifaceted role that Russia plays in contributing to the inertia surrounding these conflicts.

The first level concerns Russian peacekeeping operations. The deployment of Russian peacekeeping forces in South Ossetia, Abkhazia, and the PMR between June 1992 and May 1994 reflected Russia's forceful reengagement throughout the former Soviet Union after an initial period of neglect.[61] Russian operations were deployed to reestablish various degrees of hegemony over the new states on Russia's borders. In particular, Russia sought to compel Chisinau and Tbilisi to accede to Russian demands on a variety of questions, ranging from their membership in the CIS to forward-basing rights.

Support for the separatist movements played a critical role in the Russian strategy in the early 1990s, and peacekeeping forces were deployed after the direct involvement of Russian troops already present in these conflict zones. Under Aleksandr Lebed, the Russian 14th Army provided support to the armed forces of the PMR in May and June 1992. The Slavic officer corps also helped to create, train, and equip the PMR forces.[62] In Georgia, Russian forces were deployed along the Inguri River in June 1994. The initial peacekeeping deployment was drawn from Russian forces already in the conflict zone that had provided support to Abkhaz forces in the war. This assistance included the provision of arms and equipment, the limited participation of Russian officers and troops in combat, and even Russian air strikes against Georgian artillery positions in early 1993.[63]

The fact that Russian peacekeeping forces played a partial role in the conflict, supporting either one or the other side, remains at the forefront of the security calculations of the conflicting parties. As a result, the peacekeeping operations have tended not to promote trust between the parties but to reinforce a prevailing sense of distrust. The Moldovan government's confidence in the security guarantee provided by the peacekeeping forces has been undermined by Russia's previous support to the PMR military and Russia's permissive attitude toward the construction by the PMR of border posts in the security zone in violation of the peacekeeping agreement. In Georgia, any trust that Tbilisi might have had in the CIS (and Russian-dominated) peacekeeping operation has been destroyed by its failure to provide security for IDPs returning to the Gali district.

Russian peacekeeping troops guard the new borders separating the parties. These new borders have allowed the separatist authorities to get on with state building while the presence of Russian troops deters the metropolitan states from large-scale aggression. Moreover, Russian peacekeepers have undertaken very limited roles in the conflict zones, barely leaving their static posts on the ground.[64] Russia's approach to peacekeeping in the PMR and South Ossetia has created a built-in bias in favor of the separatists in the daily management of the peacekeeping operations. The operation in Moldova is a case in point. The peacekeeping operation was deployed in 1992 with the consent of Moldova and the separatists. The operation is tripartite, with troops from Russia, Moldova, and the PMR.[65] Moreover, it is directed through weekly meetings of a Joint Control Commission, in which Russia, Moldova, and the PMR have equal rights. The OSCE and Ukraine also participate as observers. This peacekeeping arrangement has become part of the problem. On the ground, the peacekeeping troops maintain static posts, which has allowed the PMR to deploy additional "security forces" in the security zone and done nothing to halt smuggling. Moreover, the right of veto accorded to the PMR in the Joint Control Commission has prevented the OSCE for assuming a more extensive role.

It is worth examining briefly the curiosity that is Russian peacekeeping. In theory, Russian peacekeeping concepts can be compared with the international approaches to peace support that emerged in the second half of the 1990s in Europe and elsewhere.[66] In practice, there are major differences between Russian and international peacekeeping operations—notably in the ad hoc nature of Russian operations and their lack of standard rules of engagement and timetables for withdrawal. As already noted, Russian operations have integrated the warring parties into the operations themselves. In addition, Russia has made use of troops already deployed in or around a conflict zone as peacekeeping forces. In Moldova, the former 14th Army (now a much-reduced Russian Operational Group) has adopted a peacekeeping role despite having a history of supporting Transnistrian separatist forces. In Abkhazia, the Russian airborne regiment deployed in Gudauta before the war lay at the heart of the peacekeeping operation set up in 1994. These arrangements mark the postcolonial nature of Russian peacekeeping, with troop compositions reflecting the legacy of the Soviet armed forces scattered throughout the former Soviet Union.

The fact that its troops were already stationed near conflict zones allowed Russia to react quickly to the crises in Moldova and Georgia and attenuated some of the problems usually associated with foreign troops being deployed in conflicts with little or no knowledge of the local language and culture. However, this proximity has also created problems, as Russian forward deployments are closely tied to their local communities. In the case of the former 14th Army, some of the support provided to the PMR movement by the Russian military can be explained by the fact that many officers' and soldiers' families live on the left bank. The problems in Abkhazia are different. Russia's initial peacekeeping force was drawn partly from the airborne regiment deployed in Abkhazia and partly from troops stationed in Georgia as part of the Group of Russian Forces in the Transcaucasus. The troops from Abkhazia tended to sympathize with the separatists, while the soldiers from Georgia were more supportive of the metropolitan authorities.

Russian operations are not mandated by the United Nations or the OSCE. Their legitimacy flows from the CIS imprimatur provided in the Abkhaz case and from the consent of the parties in South Ossetia and Moldova. Alongside Russian/CIS operations, the United Nations and OSCE have deployed observer missions to oversee developments in the conflicts, promote dialogue, and monitor the peacekeepers' activities. At the formal level, mechanisms of cooperation have been set up between Russian/CIS operations and international missions that include international oversight. In practice, the interaction between Russian troops and international observers on the ground has varied from slight in Moldova to significant in Abkhazia and South Ossetia.

In Moldova, the agreements between the parties on the role of the OSCE allow the few OSCE military observers to patrol the security zone and participate in the weekly Joint Control Commissions. Free movement is allowed only with prior notice to the local authorities and the peacekeeping command. Full participation in the commission also relies on the invitation of the parties. In practice, the OSCE has been limited by the reluctance of the PMR to permit significant oversight.[67] Russian-OSCE cooperation has been much more productive in South Ossetia, where the

OSCE has been integrated more deeply and actively in monitoring and in the Joint Control Commission.[68]

The final difference between Russian and international peacekeeping practice is that Russian operations are not deployed to advance "international peace and security," although this may be one of their declared secondary goals. According to Russia's Military Doctrine, first enunciated in November 1993 and reiterated ever since, Russian operations are deployed to advance Russian state interests—this is their primary objective. Troop deployments by a former imperial power in its former empire are altogether different from international peacekeeping. Russian operations have consistently sought to alter the prevailing distribution of power in these conflicts in a way that would advance Russian state interests. In short, Russian forces are more players than referees. Moreover, Russia's military presence has served to offset the weakness of the de facto state armed forces and exacerbated the weakness of the metropolitan armed forces. The balance of power on the ground is clearly strengthened in favor of the separatists.

In addition, active Russian support of the separatist forces has reinforced Moldova's and Georgia's tendency to dismiss the legitimacy of the separatists, who are seen as the fifth column of an aggressive external power. Similarly, the Azerbaijani government has refused to talk to the Nagorno-Karabakh authorities, insisting that the negotiations be held with the Armenian government in Yerevan as the real power behind the war. These circumstances have reinforced the propensity of the conflicting parties to seek an external mediator that will support their view, a savior that will allow them to fulfill their maximal aims. The situation has also muddied the picture for elites on the ground in terms of their understanding of the nature of peacekeeping, which they confuse with NATO air operations over Kosovo in 1999 and with Chapter VII UN peace-enforcement operations.

Moscow has not abandoned its strategic interests across the former Soviet Union. In particular, Russia remains intent on maintaining some military presence in Moldova and Georgia—as demonstrated in Russia's delays in withdrawing its bases from these two states, despite the agreements within the OSCE to do so. Some governments of the metropolitan states have played on this Russian ambition in order to obtain Russian support for their objectives. The separatist authorities have also exploited this Russian aim by raising the possibility that only they will allow Russia to remain in the region in the long term. In many respects, the conflicting parties adopt positions so as to benefit most from a coincidence of their own interests with Russian strategy. Overall, therefore, Russian peacekeeping operations have only increased the distrust between the parties in Moldova and Georgia and entrenched the status quo through their protection of the de facto states. In the case of Nagorno-Karabakh, where no peacekeeping forces were deployed, extensive Russian military support to its strategic ally Armenia has had a like, though lesser, effect.

Russian engagement in these conflicts has also been political. Russian governments, and especially Russia's Ministry of Foreign Affairs, have been deeply involved in negotiations to settle the conflicts. Moscow's formal position has been to support the sovereignty and territorial integrity of the metropolitan states, and for good reason—facing its own separatist conflict in Chechnya, Moscow cannot afford to support separatism in states on its borders. At the same time, Russian policies have also supported the separatist states in three different ways. First, in the early years of talks to settle the Nagorno-Karabakh conflict, Russia sought to stymie greater international involvement in the conflict. Second, Russia has put forward the concept of a "common state"—a vaguely defined confederal model for relations between the conflicting parties—as a final settlement option. From the perspective of the metropolitan capitals, this notion is seen to play largely in favor of the separatists. Third, Russia has used its position in the negotiating mechanisms to protect the position of the de facto states. This has been particularly noticeable at times in the Group of Friends of the Secretary-General, set up to foster progress in the Georgian-Abkhaz talks.

Moreover, nationalist forces in the Russian Duma, and more widely in Russian politics, have pledged support to the de facto states in Moldova, Georgia, and Azerbaijan on numerous occasions through parliamentary resolutions, public debates, and unofficial visits. The Duma has little effect on the course of Russian foreign policy. However, these activities are followed closely in the capitals of the de facto states and cited as sources of moral support, and they strengthen the determination of the separatist states, which hold out in hopes of an eventual victory of more radical forces in Russian politics. Such activities have also created a climate in which the notion, advanced by some separatist elites, of the PMR and Abkhazia some day joining into association with the Russian Federation is not ruled out.

At the economic level, the Russian government has allowed various forms of economic cooperation with the de facto states. In the PMR, the Russian Central Bank played a direct role in supporting the separatist budget in 1992 (as it did for many other non–Russian Federation subjects in the confusion of the Soviet collapse). Since then, direct support has stopped. Nonetheless, Moscow has not obstructed the numerous economic and trade agreements that have been struck between the de facto states and subjects of the Russian Federation. The PMR and Abkhazia have reached agreements with over forty members of the Russian Federation. Gazprom continues to provide energy supplies to the de facto states at basement rates. Russian private investment has occurred both in the PMR (in the steel factory, most notably) and in Abkhazia (in purchases of properties for tourism).

Russia has continued to use the de facto states to put pressure on the metropolitan states. For example, in December 2000, Russia established a visa regime on the Russian-Georgian border, which made the crossing economically prohibitive for ethnic Georgians. To Tbilisi's dismay, this regime was not applied to Russian borders with Abkhazia and South Ossetia, which are legally Georgian. Abkhazia exists thanks to its position on the Black Sea and its border with Russia. Most goods available in the market in Sukhumi, as well as Abkhazia's gasoline and gas, come across the busy border. Moreover, Abkhazia remains a part of the ruble zone. Russian support, while far less than is assumed in Tbilisi, is sufficient to sustain the existence of Abkhazia. Finally, Russia has pursued citizenship policies with the de facto states that are deeply worrying for Moldova and Georgia. In practice, Moscow has allowed people in the separatist states, most of whom retained their old Soviet passports, to register as Russian citizens and thereby receive legal travel documents. There are an estimated 65,000 Russian passport holders in the PMR and 100,000 in Abkhazia; a significant proportion of the population of South Ossetia also holds Russian passports.

As the former imperial center, Russia is not a neutral third party. In fact, it has become a party that is deeply involved at multiple levels in sustaining a status quo that serves its interests.

Other Sources of External Support: State, Substate, and Suprastate

A variety of other sources of external support help the separatist states maintain their existence. In the case of Nagorno-Karabakh, independence is really a sleight of hand barely disguising the reality that it is a region of Armenia. In February 1988, the Supreme Soviet of the Nagorno-Karabakh Autonomous Region in Azerbaijan voted to unite with the Armenian Republic. Subsequently, the independence of the Nagorno-Karabakh Republic was declared on September 2, 1991. Nagorno-Karabakh's independence allows the new Armenian state to avoid the international stigma of aggression, despite the fact that Armenian volunteers fought in the war between 1991 and 1994 and Armenian armed forces man the line of contact between Karabakh and Azerbaijan. The strength of the Armenian armed forces, and Armenia's strategic alliance with Russia, are key shields protecting the Karabakh state. Moreover, Nagorno-Karabakh has been represented in the peace talks by the Armenian president in Yerevan, Robert Kocharyan, who was the first president of the Nagorno-Karabakh Republic in the early 1990s.

Most fundamentally, the de facto state is far from self-sufficient. In the Soviet era, its economy had been deeply integrated with that of Azerbaijan and not Armenia's. The blockade instituted in 1991 cut it off from its former economic network, leading to the collapse of its economy and a near-total dependence on Armenia for most goods. This dependence is evident even in the markets in Stepanakert, which sell vegetables from Armenia. Every year the separatist authorities draw up a budget, of which they can fund only 20 to 25 percent of expenditure. Armenia then provides an annual "interstate loan" to Nagorno-Karabakh that covers the remainder of its needs. Moreover, the ministries of the de facto government have relations with the Armenian government through an extensive series of "inter-ministerial agreements." With all its needs provided for by Yerevan and unified with the Armenian legal, economic, and security space, Nagorno-Karabakh is very different from Abkhazia and the PMR, which do not have so reliable and dedicated an external patron. Crossing into Nagorno-Karabakh from Armenia through the Lachin corridor is no different from crossing an internal Armenian administrative border.

Kinship groups are another source of external support. Nagorno-Karabakh presents a unique case again. The devastating earthquake in Armenia in December 1988 sparked the rise of powerful Armenian diaspora groups to raise funds to support the people of Armenia. Nagorno-Karabakh has pride of place in the minds and hearts of the diaspora and has been the focus of intensive assistance. As a separatist area, it has been terra incognita for most international organizations. Several large diaspora organizations, such as the Fund for Armenian Relief, and in particular the Hayastan All-Armenian Fund, stepped into the vacuum to provide humanitarian assistance to the fledgling state. The Karabakh economics minister admitted in an interview in

August 2000 that most medical facilities and schools rebuilt since the end of the war had been funded by the diaspora. The reconstruction of the Karabakh state and its infrastructure has been supported through similar funds.

This support has strategic implications. The route linking the former Karabakh enclave to Armenia proper through the Lachin corridor was rebuilt with diaspora funds (and it is currently the best road in the Caucasus). In 2000, work started on the construction of a strategic road linking the southern areas and the capital to the north of Nagorno-Karabakh. Diaspora support was crucial in the early 1990s in allowing Nagorno-Karabakh to survive the difficulties of the war. Since the cease-fire, the diaspora has continued its key role in developing the infrastructure of the state at all levels, ranging from housing to public utilities. It is difficult to overestimate the role this support has played in creating Nagorno-Karabakh in material terms, as well as in acting as a pressure valve displacing any urgency for compromise with Azerbaijan.

In the PMR, kinship groups played an important role in the clashes that occurred with the Moldovan forces in 1992. In particular, hundreds of Cossacks from the Don and Kuban fought as volunteers. The Cossacks remain a pillar of support for the separatist regime. In general, the PMR has enjoyed support from a range of Slavic groups, including radical forces in Russia. The internationalist-Slavic heart of the PMR is personified in its president, Igor Smirnov, who was a factory manager in Siberia before being sent to the Dnestr region in 1985 by Moscow. Smirnov retains a Russian passport and votes in all Russian elections (reportedly always for the Communist Party).

In Abkhazia, support from ethnically related peoples in the North Caucasus was crucial in the war. The well-known Chechen commander Shamil Basayev cut his teeth in the Georgian-Abkhaz conflict, leading the International Battalion, composed of men from the North Caucasus. Basayev was nominated a Hero of Abkhazia for his actions in the war. In addition, around seventy members of the Abkhaz diaspora from Turkey fought for the

Abkhaz in the conflict. It is estimated that a few hundred Turkish-Abkhaz have returned to Abkhazia since the end of the war to live and play a part in trade with Turkey. The scale of material support that has been provided is far lower than that given to Nagorno-Karabakh by Armenians. Nonetheless, since the end of the war, related peoples in the North Caucasus have provided important moral support for the Abkhaz. The self-declared Republic of South Ossetia also benefits from support from its Russian neighbor, the North Ossetian Republic, where a large number of refugees from the war still live.

Finally, international humanitarian organizations also strengthen the status quo. Particularly in the case of Abkhazia, organizations such as the International Committee of the Red Cross, Médecins Sans Frontières, and Acción Contra la Hambre have become pillars of the separatist state. A needs assessment study conducted by the UN Development Program in Abkhazia in 1998 concluded, "A large proportion of the population receives assistance either directly or indirectly at a cost of almost 17.5 million U.S. dollars in 1997." The estimated revenue of the de facto state at the time was only U.S.$6 million. Since 1997 international support has remained at a comparable level, and the proportion of Abkhazia's population dependent on international humanitarian aid has, if anything, increased. In formal terms, international aid is several times larger than the budget of the breakaway state. A large part of the Abkhazian population survives thanks to this international support. South Ossetia is also the recipient of proportionally significant amounts of aid and support from a wide variety of sources, including UN agencies (such as the UN High Commissioner for Refugees and the World Food Program), the European Commission, the OSCE, a small number of international NGOs (including the International Rescue Committee until 2002, the Norwegian Refugee Council, and the Adventist Development and Relief Agency), and the aid and development programs of individual countries (notably, Great Britain and Switzerland).

International assistance is less important in the PMR and Nagorno-Karabakh, which have less need for basic humanitarian assistance. In Nagorno-Karabakh, however, the levels of international humanitarian support are not negligible. The aid provided by the U.S. government through the framework of Save the Children has been around $15 million per year. The assistance policies of other international organizations, such as the European Union and the European Bank for Reconstruction and Development, have also worked to entrench the current situation. For example, the European Union has committed 5 million euros to the rehabilitation of the Inguri Dam, which is the primary source of electricity generation for Abkhazia and western Georgia.

DIFFERENT LOGICS, DIFFERENT AGENDAS

The post-Soviet separatist states differ significantly from one another. These differences stem not only from differences in the root causes of each conflict but also from variations, both in absolute terms and over time, in the weight of the internal and external factors sustaining the status quo. The net result is that the de facto states are driven by different logics and have different agendas. The differences reside principally at three levels.

First, the experience of war and its impact have affected the logic driving these separatist states. The "blood spilt" factor affects how the authorities and the population within the separatist state tend to interpret the possible options for relations with the metropolitan state. The war between Moldova and the Transnistrian militias was a series of small-scale clashes in late 1991 and early 1992, culminating in the battle for Bendery in June 1992. The casualties were low, and the fighting was not communal in geographic terms: it did not pit different ethnic groups within the same village, or different villages within the same region, against one another. The experience of the war by the population was limited and restricted to specific areas. Since the 1992

cease-fire, the Transnistrian authorities have sought to elevate
the war into a mythical struggle and to depict it as a source of
legitimacy for the separatist state. The Transnistrian population,
however, does not seem to accept this interpretation. The ethnically mixed population of the left bank bears no sense of hostility toward, or desire for revenge against, the Moldovan state.
Exchanges and ties across the river have been deep and constant
almost since the day after the cease-fire.

In contrast, the wars in Abkhazia and Nagorno-Karabakh
lasted for several years and involved large-scale battles. These
wars pitted communities against each other and resulted in tens
of thousands of deaths and the displacement of hundreds of
thousands. Given the smaller size of the Armenian population in
Nagorno-Karabakh and the Abkhaz population in Abkhazia, the
impact of the war is correspondingly magnified. The experience
has profoundly affected the people living in these states, with few
left untouched. Moreover, the way these wars were conducted
has strengthened the "blood spilt" factor. The wars were fought
mostly by untrained militias and involved large-scale human rights
violations. Especially in the Georgian case, a desire for revenge
simmers in each of the affected communities—the Abkhaz in
Abkhazia and the Georgian IDPs in western Georgia. Finally, in
both Abkhazia and Nagorno-Karabakh, there is a palpable sense
of enduring threat from the metropolitan state, reinforced by
years of isolation, continuing low-level fighting, and impassioned
rhetoric from Tbilisi and Baku. The conflict between Georgian
and South Ossetian forces in the early 1990s was less prolonged
than in Abkhazia and Nagorno-Karabakh but still left lasting and
extensive physical damage in an impoverished part of Georgia.

The second principal difference between the separatist states
concerns their relationship with external sources of support.
The level and nature of this support affects the separatist authorities' degree of confidence in their ability to sustain the status
quo. The Transnistrian authorities received military support from
Russian forces at a crucial moment in 1992. More importantly,

Transnistria has received economic and commercial support from certain private groups in Russia, as well as Russian oil and gas, which has helped sustain its claim to independence. The self-declared Republic of South Ossetia has survived thanks to its position on the border with Russia, becoming over the 1990s a gateway for trafficking to and from Russia and Georgia. Nagorno-Karabakh lies in a category of its own, winning the war on the ground with Armenian volunteers and receiving the same (if not better) treatment since 1994 from Yerevan as any Armenian region. Nagorno-Karabakh has also benefited from substantial assistance from the Armenian diaspora, which has helped to rebuild the infrastructure of the separatist state. Abkhazia received important external support during the fighting with Georgian troops, but on the whole Abkhazia has never been able to rely fully on external sources of support. Since the first Chechen war, Russian policy toward Abkhazia, while not hostile, has become more ambiguous and problematic for the Abkhaz authorities. Moreover, with the outbreak of the Chechen conflicts, the Abkhaz lost a source of military support from the North Caucasus.

As a result of these differences, the economies of the de facto states have developed differently. The population in each case has become deeply impoverished. However, Transnistria has benefited from its geographic position and open borders with Moldova and Ukraine, becoming an important transit zone for goods to and from the former Soviet Union. It also inherited a few strategically important factories, which it has succeeded in developing since the Soviet collapse. Nagorno-Karabakh has survived thanks to external assistance from Yerevan and abroad. As a result, it has developed a skewed economic structure that has provided great opportunities for a few but little for a large part of the population, for whom agriculture was the mainstay. South Ossetia has become deeply impoverished since the Soviet collapse. Abkhazia must deal the most desperate situation of all, with few resources except fruits and nuts and an attractive climate for a few thousand Russian tourists who brave the blockade every summer.

These differences affect the approaches of the separatist states to negotiations with the metropolitan states. The question of the return of IDPs was never problematic for Transnistria (some 30,000 did return without problems). In South Ossetia, the return of IDPs and refugees has been delayed not so much by political obstacles as by the lack of economic opportunities in the self-declared state and the lasting damage suffered by the region. However, IDP return is a major sticking point in the negotiations for Abkhazia and Nagorno-Karabakh because of their experience of the war and their perception of the threat posed by the metropolitan state. The "blood spilt" factor has also affected the opportunities available to build economic and other ties between the metropolitan and de facto states. Abkhazia and Nagorno-Karabakh exist under blockades. These economic policies have become integrated into Georgian and Azerbaijani state policy as economic weapons against their separatist regions.

Different experiences of war have also produced differing relationships with the armed forces in the separatist states. In Abkhazia and Nagorno-Karabakh, the armed forces have pride of place and are given the lion's share of resources. Accordingly, their high commands have assumed a prominent role in the political and economic systems. In contrast, the threat to Transnistria is more internal than external. As a result, the security services have become the dominant ministry in government. The Security Ministry prevails in Transnistrian politics and economics to prevent the rise of any serious opposition, private or public, to the status quo.

The third level of difference among the states resides in the interpretation by the separatist authorities of their de facto status. Although all the de facto states have declared independence and seek formal recognition from the international community, they have different understandings of their chances of ever joining the international community and varying views on their optimal status. For Nagorno-Karabakh, the declaration of independence barely camouflages the reality of deep integration into

Armenia. Until 1991 the declared goal of the authorities in both Yerevan and Stepanakert had been unification. The collapse of the Soviet Union forced a change of strategy for Armenia, intent as a new state itself on avoiding the stigma of irredentism. The view of de facto status as a disguise covering Nagorno-Karabakh's integration into Armenia affects the scope available for a negotiated solution. Here any agreed-on settlement plan will have to compromise in some way with this reality.

In contrast, the Transnistrian authorities have become inured to the difficulties of nonrecognition and have adapted to gain the greatest benefits from it. The Transnistrian public and private authorities profit extensively from the legal limbo in which Transnistria exists and are content with retaining the freedom it provides for all sorts of criminal and unregulated activities. While Transnistrian leaders insist on retaining sovereign control over the left bank, it is uncertain that they actually seek recognition or would welcome its constraints. At various times, however, PMR authorities have raised the possibility of joining the Russia-Belarus Union. The leaders in Abkhazia are in a more difficult position, without the option of integration into Russia and not benefiting greatly from nonrecognition. As a result, the Abkhaz leaders have wavered between two maximal objectives: full recognition of their independence and association with the Russian Federation. The separatist authorities in South Ossetia have a more clearly defined vision of their independence, seeing it as a halfway house on the path toward association with the Russian Federation.

The differences among the separatist states require different approaches from an external actor seeking the settlement of these conflicts. Before exploring the scope of options available, it is worth examining the security impact of the de facto states at the local, regional, and international levels.

4

The Security Impact of the Separatist States

I N DISCUSSING THE ABKHAZ CONFLICT, the Georgian analyst Ghia Nodia argued that there exists an "impasse of volatile stability." His perspective is relevant to the other post-Soviet conflicts: "Nobody is happy, but nobody is terribly unhappy either, and life goes on. . . . Any resolute attempt to change the situation dramatically could undermine the existing—if fragile—balance, and boomerang against the initiator, so everybody is cautious."[1] This cocktail of vested interest in the present and fear of the effect of change works to strengthen the status quo. How dangerous is this situation—what effects do the de facto states have on security? These effects are both positive and negative.

The *positive impact* of the existence of the separatist states is limited. In essence, these wars are over for now. The separatists have won. In contrast to the situations in Bosnia in the early 1990s and in Kosovo in 1998 and 1999, active combat has halted in all of these conflicts. Except in the unstable Gali region, the cease-fire regimes have been respected since the early 1990s. Moreover, while weak, neither the metropolitan states nor the de facto states have collapsed along the lines witnessed in Somalia. Mechanisms of law and order are functional in all of these areas.

More broadly, a difficult situation has become increasingly nor-malized. In the Caucasus, a World Bank study of trade patterns in 2000 noted that despite the regional blockades, trade has con-tinued across the region, if still in a skewed manner. The study concluded that the effect of lifting the blockades would not be spectacular in the short term as long as the states remained insti-tutionally weak and plagued by endemic corruption: "A political settlement *per se* would not bring about immediate and drastic changes in the overall economic performance of the South Cau-casus, given the region's poor current business environment and its incomplete industrial restructuring."[2] Years after the imposi-tion of the blockades, trade has continued despite the conflicts.

Moreover, the economic difficulties of the metropolitan states do not stem only from the conflicts. They all are weak states with young and fragile political institutions facing large bureau-cracies and entrenched habits of corruption and led by politi-cians of varying competence. Moldova has become one of the poorest states in Europe; the differences between people's lives on either side of the Dnestr River are not substantial. The situa-tion in Georgia is not that much better. In the words of a Red Cross employee in Georgia: "Only one in twenty Georgians is a casualty of the conflicts. The other nineteen are victims of the economic collapse. War is not the main hardship, but economic disarray. Everything is collapsing."[3]

In addition, a form of stability has emerged on the ground in the conflict zones based on several factors. First, some of the de facto states were ethnically cleansed during the wars. There are no Georgians in Abkhazia, except in Gali, and there are no Azerbai-janis in Armenia and Karabakh. It is not to condone ethnic cleans-ing to note that these circumstances provide relative stability for now. Unlike with parts of Kosovo with a mixed population, the situation in these conflicts is closer to that of Krajina in Croatia after Operation Storm in August 1995, which forced all Serbs out of the country—the region has been stable since. Moreover, sta-bility has been maintained by a robust military deterrence system.

The armed forces of the de facto states could not be overrun by the metropolitan states on their own. The deployment of Russian peacekeeping forces has created an additional buffer against renewed conflict.

The *negative costs* of the status quo far outweigh these limited positive elements. They reside at three levels: with individuals on all sides, with the security of the metropolitan states, and with regional and wider security.

INDIVIDUAL SECURITY

In the de facto states, the average individual has been deeply affected by the conflict and its consequences. In Abkhazia and Nagorno-Karabakh, almost every family has been touched by the war through personal loss or some form of abuse experienced during the conflict. The standard of living in all of the separatist areas, which was high before the wars, has dropped catastrophically. The economies of the separatist states barely function, and the populations have suffered from widespread impoverishment and a collapse of social services and education. For most people, life has retreated to basic survival tactics of subsistence farming and shuttle cross-border trade.

The blockades and trade restrictions imposed on Abkhazia and Nagorno-Karabakh have heightened the difficulties facing the individual. In a report to the Security Council in April 1997, the UN secretary-general stated that "the serious economic and social problems in Abkhazia have been exacerbated by the region's isolation from the international community." The Abkhaz, in particular, are deeply isolated from the rest of the region and the wider world. For much of the 1990s, there was no telephone link to the outside world and the breakaway state was cut off from the positive resources of globalization such as the Internet. Without recognized passports (until the late 1990s, when Russian ones began to be provided), the Abkhaz were forced to bribe their way across the Russian border. All these difficulties have

created a profound sense of psychological isolation, which prevents the traumatic experience of the war from being assuaged. As
one member of Abkhaz civil society put it, "We live in a reserve!"

In Nagorno-Karabakh, public disaffection has translated
into disenchantment with the political leadership of the breakaway state, which is widely seen as corrupt and incompetent.
These feelings run high outside the capital, Stepanakert, but
even among the urban elites discontent is strong. In late 2000,
Grigory Afanasyan from the Karabakh State University declared:
"What is our leadership thinking of? Does it really not see that
the country is rolling toward an abyss? We have lost all sense of
morality and basic social justice. Such nations [as ours] are fated
to disappear. Such independence [as ours] is just a captivating
but empty chimera."[4]

In the de facto states, life has become desperate. Individuals
who could leave, mainly young people and those with relatives
abroad, have done so. The bulk of the remaining population
lives in penury. In Abkhazia, the Russian section of the population, mostly pensioners, is most vulnerable, lacking the family
and clan networks that ensure the survival of the Abkhaz and
the Armenians. This vulnerability is also reflected at the level of
physical security. As described by the leader of the Armenian community in Abkhazia, criminals who touch an Armenian receive
swift retribution. In a state where the law is largely absent, clan
protection makes all the difference. The experience of the war
and of the isolation that followed it has created circumstances of
impunity from crime and injustice. As a member of the United
Nations Association of Abkhazia argued, once human rights are
no longer protected, "once these elements of society are weakened, there naturally arise other tendencies, toward lawlessness
and the idea that force should prevail over the law . . . and it is
no secret that if you are brought up in primitive conditions, you
will grow up wild."[5]

Over a million people were expelled from their homes during the wars. The 700,000 IDPs in Azerbaijan and the 250,000

IDPs in Georgia still suffer the consequences of the wars despite years of cease-fire. In both countries, these displaced persons and refugees have not been integrated into the local societies and continue to live in terrible conditions. The bulk of Georgian IDPs are based in the main towns of western Georgia, with an estimated sixty thousand living in the capital, Tbilisi. As in Azerbaijan, this population remains isolated from the wider society and is largely dependent on assistance for survival. What were designed as temporary crisis management measures have become permanent fixtures of despair. In response to this situation, the United Nations designed a "New Approach" in Georgia in August 2000 to integrate the refugee population more permanently into local economies and Georgian society through income-generation support and other measures. Thus far, this change of strategy has had limited effect. The existence of compact IDP groups reinforces their sentiment of difference and also strengthens a distinct IDP view of the war, which makes potential Georgian and Azerbaijani compromise all the more difficult to achieve.[6]

SECURITY OF THE METROPOLITAN STATES

The existence of large IDP populations and the loss of substantial national territory constitute serious security threats to the post-Soviet metropolitan states. At the most basic level, the IDPs are a drain on the resources of the new states; in addition, the loss of the separatist areas has serious economic costs. In the rural country of Moldova, the loss of the PMR has left the new state devoid of real industrial potential, all energy-generating capacity, and most of the transportation links to the CIS market. The privatization effort of the Moldovan government has been overshadowed by the reality that most profitable enterprises sit across the Dnestr River. The Abkhaz region before the war provided substantial revenue from tourists, which has now been lost for the Georgian state. More generally, the existence of separatist states on their territory has been an obstacle to extensive foreign direct investment in the metropolitan states because of the risk factor and the potential for renewed conflict.

The rise of criminal structures profiting from the conflicts has undermined the new states at several levels. The smuggling opportunities offered by the de facto states have led to the loss of millions of dollars of potential state revenue in duties on the sale of cigarettes and alcohol and the import of oil and gas. A less direct result has been the increasing criminalization of the metropolitan state, with corruption and graft spreading throughout society. The de facto states are not directly responsible for this, but they have contributed to the climate of impunity prevalent throughout the metropolitan states. The existing losses, as well as the opportunity costs, are difficult to overestimate and have severely impeded the economic transition of the new states of Moldova, Georgia, and Azerbaijan.

Moreover, in each of the metropolitan states there are relatively powerful political groups with extremist views on the conflicts, which place enough pressure on the Georgian and Azerbaijani governments to block serious compromise. In Azerbaijan, as President Aliyev moved close to an agreement with Armenia, the opposition, especially the Popular Front and Musavat, coalesced to block further progress, forcing Aliyev to halt the negotiations in mid-2001. In Armenia, President Kocharyan faced a quieter but no less serious opposition to a peace deal from the Armenian Revolutionary Federation and other radical groups. The continuing existence of the separatist challenges within their borders has kept extremism alive in Georgian and Azeri politics to a degree no longer present in other post-Soviet states, which have moved on from the heady nationalist days of the early 1990s.

Finally, the existence of heavily armed separatist areas on their territory poses a direct security threat to metropolitan states. These separatist areas have allowed internal threats to connect with external challenges to the new post-Soviet states, as the conflicts have represented opportunities for hostile third parties. In Abkhazia and the PMR, Russian military troops intervened coercively in favor of the separatist forces. In Nagorno-Karabakh, Russian military support of the Armenian armed forces had a similar effect on Azerbaijan. These conflicts have allowed third parties to pressure the metropolitan state into accepting various forms of external influence, such as forward basing of Russian troops and equipment and participation in CIS collective security arrangements. The nonsettlement of these conflicts casts doubts over the entire transition process undertaken by the newly independent states.

REGIONAL AND INTERNATIONAL SECURITY

The nonsettlement of the conflicts and the blockades have exacerbated the economic situation throughout these regions. In the Caucasus, the blockades against Nagorno-Karabakh and Abkhazia have skewed economic interactions across the region by blocking rational transportation routes, barring obvious trading partners, and increasing transportation costs. A study by the World Bank in 2000 concluded that lifting these impediments to free trade in the Caucasus would increase Azerbaijan's gross domestic product by approximately 5 percent and Armenia's by as much as 30 percent in the immediate future.[7] In a region where macroeconomic stability has not led to improvement of people's lives, the opening of borders for free trade could make a substantial contribution to the economic transition of these states and alleviate the general poverty of the population.

Linked to this, the no-man's-land status of the de facto states has reinforced their criminalization. In many ways, these separatist areas have no choice but to pursue illegal economic activities, as their very existence is not legally recognized. Their authorities exploit the fact that they are under no obligation to abide by international law or trade agreements. In the case of the PMR, this was seen in the dumping of steel from the Rybnitsa steel factory across the U.S. market.

More than this, the separatist states have become focal points for regionally significant criminal activities that affect all neighboring states. South Ossetia survives as a major smuggling route to and from the North Caucasus. In Abkhazia, it has become clear that Abkhaz, Armenian, and Georgian criminal groups, in many cases with the complicity of Georgian police elements, undertake most criminal activities cooperatively. In an interview in August 2000, an anonymous member of UNOMIG remarked that in western Georgia, "the Georgian partisans are the criminals are the partisans are the criminals." A tightly knit web of illegal profit and corruption links all the main actors across the Inguri River separating Abkhazia from Georgia proper, including the Abkhaz militia, Georgian partisans, and Russian peacekeeping forces, who take their share of goods crossing the river.

The regional impact of criminal activities is particularly poignant in the PMR, which is a deeply criminalized state. The PMR represents one long open border on both its western and eastern front for the transfer of all sorts of goods and persons to and from Moldova into Romania and Ukraine. Moldovan press reports have estimated that close to two-thirds of all cigarettes sold in Moldova enter the country from the PMR, thereby allowing the importers to evade excise tax. The region is also a source of gas and oil smuggling to Moldova. On the Ukrainian border with the PMR, some U.S.$15 million in fines were imposed in 1999 against attempts to cross the border illegally. According to Ukrainian president Leonid Kuchma, the value of the goods that cross without paying tax represents a very significant loss of revenue for Ukraine.[8] In April 1999, the Moldovan deputy premier stated that the PMR "represents an epicenter for organized crime in the entire region . . . criminal structures use [the PMR] for the uncertified and wide scale transit of excisable goods."[9] The European Union is concerned directly by having the open sore of the PMR on its eastern border; Moldovan citizens have easy passage into Romania, and the number of Moldovans applying for Romanian citizenship (already estimated at 300,000) is on the increase.

Another regional-level concern is the direct military threat posed by the de facto state. The former Soviet 14th Army was based largely in the Dnestr region, where it amassed huge stocks of weapons and military equipment. In October 1994, the Russian government agreed to withdraw all of this equipment, along with the Russian troops, within two years after the ratification of the agreement by the Russian Duma. The Duma has not ratified the agreement. However, in October 1999, at the OSCE Istanbul summit, Russia agreed to withdraw or destroy the equipment by the end of 2002. Since then, a number of trainloads of equipment have been shipped to Russia. Even so, the quantities of matériel remaining in the separatist region are deeply disturbing. In June 1999, William Hill, then OSCE ambassador to Moldova, stated bluntly that "the large quantities of weapons in Transnistria, whose powers are equal to two bombs that destroyed Hiroshima, endanger the situation in the region and European security."[10]

The security impact has been more marked in the Caucasus. The de facto states of Abkhazia, South Ossetia, and Nagorno-Karabakh have been stimuli for the militarization of the region. The Caucasus remains a regional security system in formation, whose dividing lines are becoming visible. On one side, the Russian Federation has developed a military alliance with Armenia and retains a military presence in Georgia as well as in Abkhazia and South Ossetia. On the other side, Azerbaijan and Georgia have developed close military ties with Turkey, Germany, the United Kingdom, and the United States and are active participants in the NATO Partnership for Peace program. The de facto states are not the primary causes of this emerging system but a reflection of it—these areas are exploited as fissures in the nascent security system. The nonsettlement of the conflicts, therefore, has exacerbated regional tensions and increased the geopolitical struggle for influence in the area.

The final impact resides at the wider international level. The international community has become engaged in seeking to settle these conflicts. In South Ossetia and the PMR, the OSCE has served as a forum for negotiation and interaction between the conflicting parties. The peace talks in Nagorno-Karabakh have been directed by the OSCE Minsk Group and led by its three permanent cochairmen, from France, the United States, and Russia. In Abkhazia, the United Nations has taken the lead in the negotiations through the person of the special representative of the secretary-general and with the support of various UN agencies, including UNOMIG, as well as the Russian Foreign Ministry. While commendable, the involvement of this varied group of agencies has done little to advance conflict settlement. Moreover, international policy has been contradictory, with different strategies adopted for different conflicts.

The lack of progress has a cost. The case of Abkhazia is indicative of the increasing disenchantment of local politicians and societies with the international community. As an organization representing sovereign states, the United Nations has not provided direct support to the Abkhaz regime. The UN observer mission was deployed in the security zone to monitor the activities of the Russian/CIS peacekeeping forces. The Georgian government welcomed these UN policies initially. However, Tbilisi has become disenchanted with the United Nations. UNOMIG has done nothing to ensure the safety of the Georgian IDPs who have returned to their homes in the Gali district, and UN observers have failed to prod the CIS into taking a more active role in the security zone. The passivity of the United Nations was painfully evident for the Georgian government in May 1998, when Abkhaz forces swept through the Gali district, ejecting thirty thousand Georgians from their homes for a second time while UN observers watched from cover. The Georgian government and people are well aware of the actions taken by NATO in Operation Deliberate Force to halt the humanitarian catastrophe in Kosovo.

Apparent double standards and the international community's failure to act in Georgia have increased public disappointment.

In circumstances of economic duress and political instability, this disenchantment with the international community may become ingrained and may dampen public support for the overall transition process under way in these states. The failure of the international community to advance conflict settlement in the de facto states may undermine hopes that the post-Soviet region can be transformed from an area of instability and insecurity into a stable zone on Europe's periphery.

5

Ways Out

WHAT SHOULD BE DONE with these separatist states? This discussion examines traditional approaches of the international community to separatist states and the policies that have been pursued thus far toward the post-Soviet cases. Then it explores measures that might be taken to advance conflict settlement. The reality of the de facto states and the conflicts is not easy to grasp as it has become masked, even lost, in the conflicting parties' rhetoric of victory and defeat, their claims about original inhabitants and new settlers, and mutual charges of ethnic cleansing and genocide. The current status quo is deeply entrenched, and it is worth stating from the outset that these conflicts may not be settled for generations to come. However, the premise of this argument is that any settlement will have to be based on current reality on the ground and not that stemming from the source of the conflicts.

TRADITIONAL APPROACHES TO DE FACTO STATES

Scott Pegg contends that the international community has traditionally responded in one or more of three ways to separatist states: "actively opposing them through the use of embargoes and sanctions; generally ignoring them; and coming to some sort of limited acceptance and acknowledgment of their presence."[1] To these three approaches one may add a fourth option, usually adopted only by metropolitan states: active opposition and the attempt to eliminate the de facto state by force.

The treatment of the Turkish Republic of Northern Cyprus illustrates the first approach: active economic opposition. The TRNC has long been subject to embargoes imposed by the Greek Cypriots and, subsequently, a host of international organizations, including a ban on the import of TRNC produce into the European Union. The second option—simply ignoring the existence of a de facto state—has often been taken. For instance, the Provisional Government of Eritrea received this treatment in the early 1990s, before a referendum was held on independence, and the Republic of Somaliland has likewise been consistently ignored, despite the fact that, in empirical terms, the state of Somalia has hardly existed for years. The third approach is well illustrated by the case of Taiwan. At the juridical level, Taiwan has not been recognized by the international community (although some twenty-nine countries have recognized it). In practice, however, Taiwan has developed strong ties with the international community and a range of key states thanks to its own pragmatism (it has accepted being called "Taipei, China" in international fora) and the privatization of its diplomatic relations. For example, relations with the United States are directed through the American Institute in Taiwan and the Coordination Council for North American Affairs.

Operation Storm is an example of the fourth approach to de facto states: forceful action to eliminate the state. In August 1995, Croatian forces launched a whirlwind offensive against the Serbian self-declared state of Krajina inside Croatian territory, which overran the de facto state in four days and expelled some 100,000 Serbs from Croatia. The operation was undertaken with the tacit support of the international community, after years of unofficial military assistance to the Croatian armed forces by certain members of the North Atlantic alliance. Active elimination is not a policy embraced openly by the international community. However, such measures taken by metropolitan states within their own borders may be greeted with, if not always tacit support, then at least a blind eye from the international community. For example, a number of states and international organizations have raised serious concerns about the conduct of Russian troops in the second Chechen war but without questioning Russia's right to restore its territorial integrity and sovereignty.

The start of the second Chechen war of the 1990s in September 1999 is, indeed, an example of the forceful approach taken by a metropolitan state to a separatist challenge within its borders.[2] A variety of Russian federal forces have since eliminated the structures of the Chechen de facto state that had been put in place during the "Khasavyurt interim." Moscow has also rejected the legitimacy of the presidential elections of January 1997, conducted under international supervision, which had ushered Aslan Maskhadov into office. Moreover, the Russian president, Vladimir Putin, has masked the policy of eliminating the separatist threat by characterizing Russia's actions as part of the struggle against international terrorism. Therefore, any notion that the Chechen demand for greater sovereignty might be legitimate has been thoroughly rejected, and extreme measures have been taken to destroy residual elements of Chechen autonomy.

There are few examples of de facto states being accepted by the international community into the club of sovereign states. The authorities of the post-Soviet de facto states often point to the case of Eritrea, which after twenty years of armed struggle with Ethiopia was welcomed with international recognition in 1994. However, the circumstances of the Eritrean case are idiosyncratic. First, Eritrea's success was based on a demonstration by the de facto state of clear military ability. Second, and more important, its acceptance by the international community was made possible by the moderate and inclusive policy adopted in 1991 by Ethiopian president Meles Zenawi, who opened the path for the international recognition for Eritrea. In general, the international community does not recognize de facto states. Secession is usually condemned on one or more of five grounds:

- a fear of endless secession (the domino theory);
- a fear that minorities will be trapped within the new states;
- recognition of the problems of dividing assets and resources between states;
- concern for the effects of secession on democracy and civil society; and
- a fear of the proliferation of weak states in the international system.[3]

Faced by a growing number of secessionist struggles since the end of the Cold War, the international community has not become any more willing to endow de facto states with sovereignty, but it has sought to extend its options beyond the four outlined above. In particular, it has sought new ways to somehow engage separatism and recognized sovereignty. Over the course of the 1990s, the Balkan region was a crucible of innovative, if not always successful, thinking on how to square the circle of self-determination and sovereignty. The agreement reached at Dayton on ending the Yugoslav wars created the new state of Bosnia and Herzegovina from the combination of three constituent peoples, Croat, Bosniac, and Serb. This new state is composed of two entities—the Federation of Bosnia Herzegovina and the Republika Srpska—recognized and acting as a single unit under international law, and maintaining common symbols and citizenship. State institutions include a House of Peoples, a House of Representatives, a three-member presidency, and a Constitutional Court (with three members from the European Court of Human Rights), all with a careful mix of representation. The new state is a giant experiment in power sharing forced on three peoples residing inside distinct areas. In the words of one critical commentator in 2000, the result is "three de facto monoethnic entities, three

separate armies, three separate police forces, and a national government that exists mostly on paper."[4] Some progress has been
made in the areas of finance and customs toward making power
sharing work in the new state. However, this progress—indeed,
the very existence of this state as such—depends on an overwhelming presence of international troops and European admini-
strators on the ground, all working within the context of trying
to paint the country "blue and gold" and shove it on the path
toward association with the European Union.[5]

In other Balkan states, the international community has
preferred to fudge the question of marrying separatism with sovereignty. Kosovo is a case in point. Between 1989 and 1998, the
underground "Republic of Kosova" coexisted with the central
Serbian authorities, creating a range of parallel institutions of
statehood and independence.[6] NATO launched Operation Deliberate Force in 1999 in response to the actions of the Yugoslav
army in the region, which in turn were prompted by a failure to
find a solution between competing Kosovar and Serbian demands.
Since the war, the international community has pointedly
ignored discussing the end status of Kosovo, even if the empirical
reality on the ground points to the creation of a de facto independent Kosovar state.

A recent addition to the Balkan cauldron of fudged states is
the creation of the new State Union of Serbia and Montenegro
in early 2003, which marks the final passing into history of Yugoslavia. This State Union is designed to reconcile Montenegrin
demands for independence with Serbian insistence on territorial integrity, all within the framework of international reticence
to countenance the birth of new states without the consent of all
parties concerned. At the same time, provisions envisage the
possibility of the eventual separation of the two entities, as the
new constitution allows for public referenda on separation after
three years.[7]

Another relevant example is the attempt since the end of
the Cold War to settle the Cyprus conflict through an agreement

between the TRNC and the Republic of Cyprus. The 1990s saw the introduction of a fundamentally new factor in this conflict after over thirty years of stalemate and negotiations led by the United Nations: the prospect of a reunited island of Cyprus becoming a full member of the European Union. With this objective on the horizon, Secretary-General Kofi Annan launched an intensive series of negotiations and proximity talks between 1999 and 2003 to secure a comprehensive peace agreement. Annan's proposed Basis for the Comprehensive Settlement of the Cyprus Problem[8] included a foundation agreement for the creation of a United Cyprus Republic (which would have a "federal government" and would be composed of two constituent states) that was to be submitted to referendum on both parts of the island. It was hoped that the overall change of context resulting from the promise of EU accession would secure agreement on the UN proposal. Deadlines for talks and the referenda were tied to the culmination of EU enlargement in 2004.

The process stumbled for a number of reasons. First, the Turkish Cypriot leadership, under Rauf Denktash, refused to cede on a number of sticking points that concerned the future "sovereignty" of the Turkish constituent state of United Cyprus, including the right to some international legal status and the right to secede. Second, the EU carrot of accession did not have all of the expected effects and even had unexpected ones.[9] The assumption that the promise of membership and economic support would override political aspirations in the TRNC proved unfounded—for now at least. Moreover, as Thomas Diez has noted, the European Union failed to present itself as a neutral outside party in the conflict, given Greek membership in the Union, the Union's sometimes troubled ties with Turkey, and the Union's recognized state-bias toward the Greek Republic of Cyprus. Nonetheless, the progress achieved since 1999 is impressive. A number of fundamental points have been accepted in the talks on how to combine the sovereignty of the two parts of the island under a common state structure. Especially given the changing relations of the European Union with Turkey, and in particular with the Turkish government elected in late 2002, a settlement seems closer than ever before.

CURRENT APPROACHES IN THE FORMER SOVIET UNION

European states, the United States, Russia, and international organizations have approached post-Soviet de facto states in a range of ways. Inconsistency has become the hallmark of these efforts, with the same actors adopting different approaches to the region as a whole and with different actors trying different policies toward the same de facto state. Thus far, four approaches have been tried: *attacking* the de facto state (an option adopted only by metropolitan states), *embargoing* it, *engaging* with it, and *ignoring* it. Table 1 charts these efforts. The actors involved include the metropolitan states (MS); important third parties, notably, Russia, the United States, and diasporas (3P); intergovernmental organizations, including the United Nations, the European Union, and the OSCE (IO); international nongovernmental organizations such as the International Committee of the Red Cross and Médecins Sans Frontières (INGO); and international financial institutions (IFI).

All the metropolitan states sought in the first instance to eliminate the de facto states. The level of force ranged from limited in Moldova to considerable in Azerbaijan. Forceful measures failed. There is little reason to believe that any of the metropolitan states will in the medium term be capable of overrunning the separatist states. The Moldovan armed forces are very weak. While numerically larger, the Georgian and Azerbaijani armed forces are not combat-ready, having suffered from a decade of underfinancing and civilian distrust. Moreover, while very small, the armed forces of the de facto states are significant adversaries, with combat-experienced troops, substantial political support, and a determined reserve base. Russia's presence in peacekeeping operations in Moldova and Georgia provides additional

Table 1. International Approaches toward the De Facto States

	Attack	Embargo	Engage	Ignore
PMR	*Actor: MS*	*Actors: IFI + IO*	*Actors: MS + RF + IO*	*Actors: IO + MS*
	■ 1992, clashes	■ No IFI assistance ■ No bilateral aid	■ Economic relations with MS and Russia ■ Private trade (e.g., steel to United States) ■ Talks with Moldova since 1992 ■ Indirect Russian military assistance	■ Nonrecognition
Abkhazia	*Actor: MS*	*Actors: CIS + IFI + IO + MS*	*Actors: RF + INGO + IO + MS*	*Actors: IO + MS*
	■ 1992, attack ■ 1997–, sabotage actions by "partisans"	■ CIS sanctions ■ No IFI support ■ No direct bilateral aid ■ Russian border regime ■ Georgian blockade	■ Relations with subjects of Russian Federation ■ INGO assistance ■ EU assistance (Inguri Dam project) ■ Talks with Georgia ■ North Caucasian support ■ Indirect Russian military assistance	■ Nonrecognition

South Ossetia	*Actor: MS*	*Actors: IFI + MS*	*Actors: RF + INGO + IO + MS*	*Actors: IO + MS*
	■ 1990–92, clashes	■ No IFI support ■ No direct central Georgian ties	■ Ties with subjects of the Russian Federation (especially North Caucasus) ■ INGO assistance programs ■ EU/OSCE/UN agency assistance programs (small-arms collection, food safety, and infrastructure rebuilding) ■ Ties with some central Georgian authorities ■ Assistance and confidence-building programs by individual states (Great Britain, Switzerland)	■ Nonrecognition
Nagorno-Karabakh	*Actors: MS*	*Actors: MS + IFI + 3P*	*Actors: INGO + Armenia + IO + 3P*	*Actors: IO + MS*
	■ 1990–94, war	■ Blockade by Azerbaijan and Turkey ■ No IFI assistance	■ INGO assistance ■ Integration with Armenia ■ Indirect U.S. assistance (via Save the Children) ■ Indirect Russian assistance (via military alliance with Armenia) ■ Diaspora assistance	■ Nonrecognition ■ No direct talks with Azerbaijan

deterrence against any designs of the metropolitan states to restore their territorial integrity by force of arms. Armenia plays a similar role in deterring Azerbaijan from attempting to recapture Nagorno-Karabakh.

Since the end of the wars, the de facto states have not been either consistently ignored or comprehensively embargoed by the international community. Through various private and nongovernmental means, the separatist states have developed ties and received assistance from a range of external actors. In the cases of the PMR and Nagorno-Karabakh, Moldova (as the metropolitan state) and Armenia (as key patron) have provided important sources of aid and outlets for trade. Limited acceptance and various forms of engagement have given the de facto states enough maneuvering room to survive over the past decade through subsistence strategies. The inconsistent approach of the international community has contributed to the entrenchment of the status quo in these conflicts.

The efforts by third parties to advance conflict resolution must be understood in light of this inconsistent wider approach. In these circumstances, peace talks have failed to produce substantial progress in any of the conflicts. Negotiations have focused on two groups of concerns: (1) the status of the separatist area and its future relations with the metropolitan center, and (2) the need to address the problems that arose from the wars themselves, such as the return of refugees and IDPs, and the withdrawal from territory occupied by separatist forces. In the talks, the de facto states have pursued an objective immediately below outright independence. All have favored the creation of a "common state" with the former metropolitan center. In each case, the concept has been interpreted differently.

In the conflict between Moldova and the PMR, formal progress has occurred toward the creation of a "common state" composed of Moldova and the PMR. In negotiations led by Russia, the two parties agreed to a memorandum to this effect in Moscow on May 8, 1997. The agreement, called On the Basis for the

Normalization of Relations between the Republic of Moldova and Transnistria (PMR), seemed to open the way for an accommodation of Moldovan demands for respect of its territorial integrity and the PMR pursuit of self-determination. The agreement stated that the parties would seek to establish "state-legal relations." In particular, Article 11 stated, "The parties shall build their relations in the framework of a common state within the borders of the Moldovan Soviet Socialist Republic as of December of the year 1990."

Since 1997, the talks have centered on defining more clearly the meaning of "common state." Differences between the parties have blocked attempts by the OSCE to determine a division of competencies within the framework of territorially integral Moldova.[10] The Moldovan government seeks federal relations in this common state, with Chisinau retaining important functions as the federal center, while federal units, such as the PMR, would have substantial devolved responsibilities. In contrast, the PMR seeks a confederal-type structure, in which there is no center as such, only two equal parties united by treaty in a voluntary association. As a result, talks have drifted between the two parties. Even with the advent of a pro-Russian communist president in Moldova, Vladimir Voronin, after the February 2001 parliamentary elections, the PMR has not become more amenable. In the words of the PMR's foreign minister, Valery Litskai, the "common state already exists." For the PMR, there is little else to achieve— the authorities are content with the limbo status in which they exist, as long as the separatist state remains connected to the world market.

Nonetheless, progress occurred in 2003 following Voronin's proposal for a joint constitutional commission with the PMR to redraft the Moldovan constitution. Tiraspol has joined this process, partly stimulated by heavy and new pressure placed on the separatist leaders by the European Union and United States acting jointly to impose a travel ban on the separatist leaders in February 2003 and raising the threat of asset seizures. Moreover, the OSCE made a formal request that the European Union consider the possibility of deploying a "peace consolidation" mission to the conflict zone to support the implementation of an agreement on a new constitutional relationship.[11] Despite these signs of progress, a settlement of the conflict will still be difficult to achieve. The separatist authorities have continued to play a waiting game in the constitutional talks. The Russian government put forward a draft settlement memorandum in November 2003 that took by surprise many in Moldova and the OSCE, not only for the weakness of its propositions—of which there were many—but also for the unilateral—some might say arrogant—manner in which it was delivered.

Ten years of negotiations on the conflict in Abkhazia have yielded no significant success. An impression of progress was created in June and July 1997 by a series of talks led by Yevgeny Primakov and the Russian Foreign Ministry. According to the Abkhaz foreign minister, Sergei Shamba, an agreement on building a common state between Georgia and Abkhazia was abandoned at the last minute because of Georgian hesitations. Following this, the UN special representative of the secretary-general has taken the lead in the negotiations. Between 1997 and 1999, the special representative focused on developing confidence-building measures between the two parties through joint working groups on security, economic, and refugee issues. As little progress occurred at these levels, the United Nations turned once again, in 1999–2000, under the leadership of Special Representative of the Secretary-General Dieter Boden, to discussions on the two central issues blocking progress: the status of Abkhazia and its relationship to Tbilisi, and the return of Georgian IDPs to Abkhazia under the so-called Boden Plan.

No progress was made on either issue, although the Abkhaz government decided unilaterally in 2000 to allow Georgian IDPs to return to the Gali district (but without adequate security guarantees or international support). With regard to future relations with Georgia, the Abkhaz position has hardened to an absolute refusal to discuss the question of Abkhazia's status, as this might imply a subordinate position inside Georgia. The Abkhaz authorities insist that they are prepared to discuss only the question of establishing a treaty relationship with Georgia based on voluntary cooperation between two sovereign states possessing equal rights. Whereas the PMR authorities are content with the current limbo status enshrined in the 1997 common state agreement, the Abkhaz perspective is different. For Sukhumi, the concept of a common state with Georgia represents an interim position that would prepare the already sovereign Abkhazia for juridical independence. With good reason, Tbilisi fears that after an agreement on some form of common state, Sukhumi would quickly abrogate treaty-based equality for full independence, leaving Tbilisi with no leverage over Abkhazia and no solution to its IDP problem. In 2003, talks resumed on a range of phased confidence-building measures. Interestingly, Russia has created a new negotiation track, based around the Russian and Georgian presidents (the so-called Sochi process), that works in parallel with the UN tracks. Georgia's Rose Revolution of November 2003 has thrown into the air all previous policies toward Abkhazia. The new leadership in Tbilisi is clearly nationalist—and at times populist—yet its overriding priority is to rejuvenate the Georgian state, and thus it is unlikely to distract itself from that task by acting rashly toward Abkhazia. Most likely, Tbilisi will pursue a holding policy in the settlement talks.

Talks in South Ossetia have occurred on two tracks since 1992. The first track has consisted of talks on an overall political settlement between the parties, a settlement that would involve Russia, the OSCE, and North Ossetia. These talks have produced no progress on the resolution of the political status of the breakaway state. In fact, since the election of Eduard Kokoyev as president in 2001, the South Ossetian line has hardened against compromise on the status question. Increasing noise is heard from the separatist capital Tskhinvali about a future association with the Russian Federation.

The second track has been far more successful. Led by the Joint Control Commission, and with financial assistance and technical expertise from international organizations, especially the OSCE and the European Union, the two parties have established pragmatic relations in the course of the past decade. The Joint Control Commission contains working groups on military and security questions, economic issues, and the concerns of refugees and IDPs. The return of refugees and IDPs has been slow, mainly because of the lack of economic opportunities in South Ossetia—indeed, the self-declared state is being depopulated as young people leave to find work elsewhere. The security situation has been stable for the past decade. The international community has engaged in a number of small-scale but relatively successful confidence-building and infrastructure-rebuilding programs. Since 1998, for example, the European Union has been involved in repairing the region's railway lines.

In 2000, the Georgian and South Ossetian parties agreed to create, with OSCE and EU assistance, a Joint Law Enforcement Coordination Body to address the breakaway region's rampant criminality. Overall, relations on the ground between Georgians and South Ossets are normal; ties have also been built between the separatist and central authorities. However, for all the pragmatism displayed by both parties and the engagement of the international community, progress toward a settlement at the political level has been elusive—and none can be expected until the Georgian-Abkhaz conflict is settled.

In the first years of talks on Nagorno-Karabakh, Russia and the OSCE adopted clashing approaches to the conflict, which obstructed all progress beyond the cease-fire agreement of 1994. Only since a consensus emerged among all third parties has progress been possible.

Until 1995, Russia and the OSCE Minsk Group led parallel negotiations between Armenia and Azerbaijan over the conflict in Nagorno-Karabakh. These circumstances allowed a cease-fire regime to be initiated (secured by Russia) and some humanitarian assistance to be delivered to Karabakh. However, the parallel talks failed to address the central concerns of the two parties. Azerbaijan's central concerns are to restore sovereign control over its territory (which requires not only the withdrawal of Karabakh forces from the occupied territories but also their demobilization inside the Karabakh region itself), to secure the return of Azerbaijani IDPs to their homes, and to establish a division of powers with Karabakh that would leave Baku sovereign. Armenia's primary aims are to retain a land tie with Karabakh through the Lachin corridor, to ensure the security of Nagorno-Karabakh, and to develop a horizontal relationship between Stepanakert and Baku.[12] After 1997, the positions of Russia and the OSCE became more coordinated, and the Minsk Group became the central negotiating forum.[13] Between May 1997 and November 1998, the Minsk Group produced three different drafts for a comprehensive settlement of the conflict, which sought to address various aspects of each party's position. The last draft in late 1998 followed the lines of the common state concept developed in Moldova and Georgia. The Azerbaijani president rejected this proposal as an affront to his country's territorial integrity and a sop to Armenian aggression.

Subsequently, the talks shifted to bilateral meetings between President Heydar Aliyev and President Robert Kocharyan. After several years of such direct meetings, the format of the talks shifted again in 2001. In a summit in February 2001, organized and led by French president Jacques Chirac, a number of socalled Paris Principles were hammered out between the two presidents. The U.S. government then held a series of proximity talks in Key West in early April, where further progress was reported.

While the content of the talks was kept confidential, the contours of the potential deal are clear.[14] The Armenians would return immediately six of the seven Azerbaijani regions they occupy outside the former Nagorno-Karabakh Autonomous Region: that is, the regions of Agdam, Fizuli, Jabrail, Kelbjar, Kubatly, and Zangelan. This withdrawal would alleviate the bulk of Azerbaijan's

IDP problem, as 80 percent of the IDPs are from these areas. A massive IDP return would take place as soon as possible with extensive international financial and material support. It is possible that Azerbaijani IDPs would also have the right to return to their homes inside Karabakh. However, this return would not be immediate, nor would it be pressed by the international community in order to avoid the security dilemmas that may arise from the mingling of the two populations. In exchange for this concession, Azerbaijan would gain internationally secured access through the Armenian Meghri region to the Azerbaijani region of Nakhichevan. In addition, the blockades of Armenia and Nagorno-Karabakh would be lifted. On the status of Nagorno-Karabakh itself, the agreement would remain purposely ambiguous. Azerbaijan will not accept any violation of its territorial integrity, and the Armenians will not allow Karabakh to be subordinated to rule from Baku. The murky result would allow Karabakh to retain a de facto status tied to Armenia while de jure remaining a part of Azerbaijan.

The talks made substantial progress, clearing the ground on most fundamental questions. The Armenian president realized the need to reach peace (under the right conditions) with Azerbaijan to lift the decade-long blockades that have strangled the Armenian economy and society. On the Azerbaijani side, Heydar Aliyev seemed to have recognized the following fundamental points. First, Nagorno-Karabakh was lost for Azerbaijan. Second, the blockades against Armenia and the separatist state had failed to bring them to their knees. Third, any attempt by Baku to negotiate Karabakh's return to some kind of autonomous status inside Azerbaijan, along the lines of the prewar situation, was unrealistic. However, the summit between Aliyev and Kocharyan planned for Geneva in May 2001 was suspended and the negotiations placed on hold. The essential problem was that neither president had devoted time to preparing their constituencies for the idea of a peace deal or for the contours of a compromise. As a result, the talks were out of sync with Armenian and Azerbaijani societies. The two presidents, political survivors first and fore-most, turned to protect their vulnerable flanks on the domestic scene. Despite the pressures of old age and his apparent desire to leave a legacy of peace and stability, Aliyev retreated from sign-ing what the opposition called a "defeatist" agreement. In Arme-nia, despite the clear advantages provided by a potential agree-ment, the radical nationalist opposition also seized the issue to attack Robert Kocharyan. The talks were put on hold until after the presidential elections in 2003 in both states.

THE POWER OF INERTIA

The two extreme approaches toward de facto states—recognition and elimination—are not feasible in the case of the post-Soviet separatist states. Outright recognition of them as sovereign states by the international community would set a dangerous prece-dent, yet the metropolitan states are unable for now to impose their will forcefully on the separatist areas. Current international and regional policies, falling between these extremes, have only entrenched the de facto states, and negotiations have produced few results. What approach might be more effective? How might the policies of the international community be made more con-sistent internally and more appropriate externally for the situa-tion on the ground?

Before answering these questions, it is worth recalling two central arguments of this study. The first concerns the strength of the status quo in these conflicts. Inertia is driven by a host of factors relating to the state-building projects of the de facto states and their interaction with a range of external actors and sources of support. The de facto states, the metropolitan states, and major third parties have entrenched interests. In this better-the-devil-you-know situation, enough groups profit enough on all sides of the front lines for the present to be acceptable; the pur-suit of compromise with adversaries for some ill-defined future carries too many dangers. These post-Soviet conflicts have become a system, with myriad levels of interaction between the system's constituent parts and with an internal logic that drives it. The collapse of the Cyprus talks, despite the promises they held for all parties, highlights the difficulty of reconciling the claims of separatist entities with the norms of sovereignty and territorial integrity. A de facto state exists of and for itself; it will not disappear for the sake of an uncertain and "common" greater good. As time passes and new generations are born and raised in the separatist and metropolitan states, the prospect of full resolution of the conflicts may recede ever further.

A second central argument advanced in this study is that the conflicts are unlikely to be settled by creating federal power-sharing structures. Proposals that feature such structures are based on premises that are absent in the post-Soviet cases. In his examination of power-sharing arrangements, Timothy Sisk argues that four conditions create success.[15] First, a core of moderate and representative politicians on either side must embrace the notion of power sharing. Second, any power-sharing arrangement must put forward flexible practices and provide for an equitable distribution of resources. Third, it must be locally driven and not imposed by external parties. Finally, the power-sharing arrangement should permit extremist actions—the use of the veto, for example—but the parties to the arrangement should refrain from exercising such options. The basic point is that such arrangements are based on a foundation of goodwill and voluntarism from the conflicting parties, who must be devoted to making the arrangements work. Moreover, the baseline context for such solutions is that of democracy, where by definition political actors agree to work within a system of institutionalized uncertainty that is made acceptable by the recognition by all of the rules of the game and of a shared sense of destiny.

The post-Soviet conflicts are seen as wars of clashing destinies that are characterized by the absence of any voluntarism and trust in the "other." The de facto states are not democratic, while the metropolitan states are democratic only to a degree.

There are moderate politicians on all sides, but they represent at best only part of their society; certainly, they do not represent a core of public opinion. As a result, any federalizing power-sharing agreement is likely to require external imposition and likely to lack a local perception of ownership. In this climate, it is unlikely that politicians will refrain from extremist actions. As in Bosnia-Herzegovina, only massive external involvement can attenuate these pressures—and then only barely. Given that all-encompassing international engagement is unlikely in the former Soviet Union, other options must be considered.[16]

EXITING IMPASSES?

The Georgian-Abkhaz conflict remains far from settlement, with little consensus among the third parties on the principles of resolution and with the conflicting parties reluctant to address central questions. However, there is scope for nudging the conflicts onto the path to settlement. A bare-bones framework has been put in place to settle the PMR conflict, and agreement has more or less been reached on many of the fundamental questions concerning Nagorno-Karabakh. The idea of creating a blueprint to resolve all the conflicts along the same lines is nonsensical. However, if external actors were to adopt more coherent policies toward the de facto states, the dynamics of these conflicts might start to change for the better. The following sections first discuss the shape of a general international coordinated strategy and then examine where and how to start a push for settlement.

It is important, before considering the contours of such a policy, to define more clearly the objectives to guide the international community. The first aim must be to preserve international order and stability. The de facto states should be recognized *only* if conditions contribute to this aim; that is, only if the metropolitan state approves its own partition. In the absence of this approval, the international community can still pursue order and stability, not through the isolation of the de facto states but through engagement with them. The isolation of the de facto states has only entrenched their recalcitrance and created opportunities for the coercive involvement of third parties. In Georgia, Abkhazia's isolation has led the de facto state to rely on Russian military support, to the detriment of Georgia's overall security. A key objective of the international community could be to neutralize the de facto states as potential levers of influence used by third parties against the metropolitan states.

The international community should also seek to reduce the pressures leading to the militarization of these regions. The dividing lines emerging in the former Soviet Union should be diminished, not accentuated. To this end, the international community should not condone the activities of "partisans" in Georgia, which are counterproductive to the parallel negotiations for a peace settlement. Linked to this, the international community could press for an end to the system of blockades in the Caucasus, which have undermined the region's prospects for economic development, blocked foreign investment, and skewed trade patterns. In security terms, they have only exacerbated a nascent and hostile alliance system. An end to the blockades and the beginning of more open relations will not automatically produce a benign region in which armed forces have no role. The point is to create a more rational and balanced deterrence system, where force plays a passive role and arms races remain under control.

The second international objective should be justice. This is a tall order. In post-conflict situations, as perhaps in all situations, justice lies in the eye of the beholder. Furthermore, the blind pursuit of this aim may undermine the objectives of order and stability. The pursuit of justice must be undertaken judiciously and with a long-term perspective. The most pressing problem related to justice concerns the fate of the IDP populations, who should have a right to return to their homes and should be given international support to exercise this right. This return is itself important to the goal of establishing order and stability.

However, it is worth considering whether this right should be immediately applicable to all parts of the de facto states.

The progress that occurred in 2001 over Nagorno-Karabakh was based on the objective of balancing order with justice. In essence, the potential agreement was to have been founded on recognition by Baku of its defeat in the war and the de facto loss of Karabakh (and this is what made Aliyev retreat at the last minute). Such a settlement would have worked with the grain of the status quo that has emerged over the past decade in terms of power arrangements on the ground. At the same time, it could have broken the existing inertia and initiated a new, more positive logic.

To achieve greater synergy of effort, it is crucial that all third parties, and the wider international community, coordinate their approaches to the de facto states. Coordination in itself is unlikely to resolve fully the question of the existence of the de facto states (recognition or elimination, of course, would bring an unambiguous resolution), but greater coordination may succeed in breaking the current inertia.

This raises two questions: *Who* can and should undertake such efforts? *Why* should they do so?

The international community is already deeply involved in these conflicts. A number of individual states, including Russia, the United States, and European states, have developed policies regarding the separatist regions. International organizations and a range of nongovernmental bodies are engaged in these areas as well. In fact, many elements of a potentially effective settlement initiative already exist. However, current external policies are not coordinated; on the contrary, they contradict one another, with some external approaches favoring engagement while others try to ignore the de facto states. The main task of an international mediator should be to coordinate current policy lines and smooth out the differences between them.

If an external actor is to play an effective role in mediating these conflicts, it must meet three criteria. First, it must have an interest in undertaking the role, no matter whether that interest is stimulated by its proximity to the conflict, by a need to protect its interests, or by other factors. Second, the external actor must feel some sense of urgency, whether driven by the prospect of peace or by the fear of an enduring status quo. Third, the external actor must be acceptable to the parties in conflict.

A number of third parties fulfill some but not all of these criteria. Russia, for one, meets the first two criteria but not the third. Another major state, the United States, may have an interest in settling these conflicts, but Washington feels little sense of urgency in shouldering the burden of mediation in these regions; furthermore, U.S. mediation would not be fully acceptable to some third parties. The OSCE has a deep interest in settling these conflicts, resulting from almost a decade of active engagement, and its multilateral approach has made it an acceptable coordinator for negotiations. However, it is arguable whether the OSCE perceives an urgent need to settle the conflicts; it is also unclear whether the organization, even if it did wish to act swiftly, could actually do so, given its weak institutional capacity and time-consuming consensual decision-making processes.

Two international organizations meet all three criteria: the United Nations and the European Union. The United Nations is already deeply involved throughout all the post-Soviet conflicts and plays a leading role in the Georgian-Abkhaz conflict. Moreover, outside the former Soviet Union, the United Nations has developed a large body of experience in addressing similar conflicts over sovereignty and territory. For example, the United Nations played an impressive role in 2002 and 2003 in efforts to resolve the conflict in Cyprus.

With its coming enlargement, the European Union has a growing interest in settling the conflicts on its new periphery. The breakdown of progress over Cyprus in 2003 highlights that, even when EU membership is offered, the European Union is not always able to settle intractable conflicts. Nonetheless, thanks partly to the role played by the European Union, the Cyprus conflict is now closer to settlement than at any point in its thirty-year history. Moreover, contingent political factors, linked to the leadership of the TRNC and the advent of a new Turkish government, go a long way in explaining why progress stalled. The long-term outlook remains encouraging, with many observers anticipating a settlement of the conflict that will see a united island of Cyprus become a member of the European Union.

The enlarged European Union's new proximity to the former Soviet Union adds real urgency to its policies toward that region. At EU headquarters in Brussels and in the capitals of member-states, there is general recognition of the need for the organization to adopt a more active policy toward its new neighbors. The draft EU Security Concept, written by High Representative Javier Solana, was accepted by the member-states in June and finalized in December 2003. The Security Concept calls for the creation of a belt of well-governed states on the European periphery. In 2002, the EU Council Secretariat began the process of defining new strategies for dealing with the European Union's periphery after enlargement; known as the New Neighborhood Initiative, the process focuses on Ukraine, Belarus, and Moldova. Discussions in the EU Council of the need to develop more effective policies toward the states on the Union's borders that do not have an immediate prospect of acceding to the organization resulted in March 2003 in the European Commission adopting a white paper titled "Wider Europe—New Neighborhood." Since December 2002, the European Union has started to adopt a more forceful presence in the Moldovan conflict and is considering the deployment of a civilian operation. Moreover, in July 2003, the European Union designated a Finnish diplomat, Heikki Talvitie, as the EU special representative to the South Caucasus, with a mandate to advance conflict settlement in the region.

The European Union not only is becoming increasingly aware of the need to engage countries on its new borders but has started to do so. Employing an expanding range of foreign policy tools to advance EU interests in its neighborhood, the

European Union is learning to become a "normal" strategic actor—something it never was in the 1990s, when its foreign policy was largely limited to offering or not offering membership.

The European Union may have the advantage over other potential mediators of being acceptable to the parties in conflict as well as to important third parties. For instance, the Russian government under Putin has been keen on forging closer ties with the European Union, especially as it develops a common foreign and security policy. An EU presence in the former Soviet Union that takes account of Russia's voice is likely to be acceptable to Moscow. Moreover, the European Union can provide a multilateral framework that would include other key states, such as the United States, France, and the United Kingdom, as well as the OSCE, the United Nations, and international financial institutions.

The second question—*why* the European Union or the United Nations should take on the role of settlement coordinator —may at first seem hard to answer. The wars over the de facto states are no longer active. Little blood is being shed. The massive exoduses caused by the conflicts have already occurred. The media visibility of these wars is nil. While the status quo is optimal neither for the metropolitan states nor for the de facto states, political and economic structures have been built that make it less painful, even sustainable.

Moreover, settlement coordination is not cheap. An external actor will have to expend significant financial, material, and, especially, political resources, in terms of will and capital. Even with such expenditures, third-party intervention might only worsen the situation, at least in the short term, by provoking the rise of extremist forces in the metropolitan states, which might in turn prompt the de facto states to make warlike moves. In short, intervention might create a vicious circle of threat and counterthreat that could derail any constructive negotiations. Other parties also might look askance at third-party involvement. The Russian government, for example, might not accept willingly or gracefully the settlement of conflicts that have given Russia leverage with its neighbors. Russia's initial reaction to the notion of an EU-led peace support operation in Moldova was barely lukewarm. And the international community as a whole might frown on a settlement that recognizes, in whatever form, the existence of the de facto states, thereby setting a precedent that might encourage separatists elsewhere.

However, the costs of the status quo already outweigh its benefits, and the price of inaction is sure to rise over time. As discussed in the previous chapter, the unresolved conflicts carry a cost at the level of the individual, in both the de facto and the metropolitan states. The status quo also undermines the economic prospects and political stability of the metropolitan state and the surrounding region, raising persistent questions about the very viability of these states. The existence of de facto states has increased regional levels of crime and smuggling, threatening the metropolitan state and the security of the wider region. The South Caucasus is a region crippled by blockades and trade restrictions, counterbalancing alliances, and arms races. Continuing the status quo poses threats also to international security. The weakness of the Georgian state was dramatically highlighted by its loss of control over the Pankisi valley, near the border with Chechnya, which was briefly used as a base for international terrorists. The possibility of failing states on Europe's border cannot be neglected by the international community.

FIVE ELEMENTS OF A COORDINATED INTERNATIONAL POLICY

A coordinated settlement policy toward these conflicts will have to confront five issues—status, IDP return, security measures, society-to-society links, and economic support—if it is to break the current inertia. Many measures addressing these issues have already been instituted, but they have been developed by different external actors and applied to different conflicts in an uncoordinated and often contradictory fashion. These measures must be woven together and action taken on all five issues simultaneously if the status quo is to be broken. For example, lifting the blockades on Abkhazia and Nagorno-Karabakh will serve only to entrench the status quo unless it is part of a wider strategy of conflict settlement. A coordinated international policy could produce more than simply synergy of effort—it could help to break the current inertia and launch a new logic of interaction between the conflicting parties on the ground.

The objective here is not to present a single grand plan for settling all the conflicts. The conflicts and their consequences are very different, and no plan could possibly suit all of them. However, the de facto states are sufficiently similar in terms of the forces driving them that the main strands of a coordinated international policy can be discerned.[17]

Status

An agreement on the status of the de facto state will have to be founded on current realities. Drawing from the Nagorno-Karabakh talks, discussions should focus on seeking to maintain the juridical integrity of the metropolitan state while recognizing the empirical existence of the de facto state.

Although the concept of the common state has been largely discredited by the Moldovan experience, the spirit of the concept is not necessarily negative. Various workable forms of association between the de facto and the metropolitan states can be developed beyond the federal or confederal models. Under such arrangements, the de facto state would not have the right to secede from the association state without the former metropolitan state's approval, and the *external* sovereignty of the de facto state would have to be diluted—for example, the metropolitan state would have sole right to international status, although the de facto state might still be allowed to entertain privileged ties with external parties. At the same time, the *internal* sovereignty of the de facto state would remain barely infringed upon by the metropolitan state, and only with its accord. The aim here should be to balance de facto and de jure sovereignty in a manner that requires all parties to compromise and generates benefits for all.

Such an agreement on status must be accompanied by agreement on the following four issues if the experience of Moldova's "common state" is not to be repeated.

IDP Return

To defuse the explosive potential of maintaining large IDP populations and to persuade the metropolitan society of the need for a compromise on status, the IDPs must return home. This return should be fully assisted by the international community. However, the return should not occur immediately inside all parts of the de facto state.

In Azerbaijan, all IDPs could return immediately to the occupied territories, but not in the short term to every part of Karabakh. In Abkhazia, Georgian IDPs could, if international protection and humanitarian support were made available, return immediately to the Gali region, where they were a compact majority before the war. In both cases, immediate, if partial, returns would alleviate the bulk of the IDP burden and avoid the mistake of forcing war-afflicted populations to restart their lives by immediately mingling with the same population whose forces played a part in expelling them originally. At the same time, the international community must fund policies that integrate the remaining IDP population into the societies and economies of the areas where they now reside. The right to full return throughout the de facto states should be endorsed by the international community but should be interpreted not as a short-term priority but over a longer period of time. Those who cannot return to their homes immediately should receive financial compensation from an internationally supported fund.

Security Measures

In each conflict, the international community must seek to negotiate regional arms-control agreements that reduce the numbers of troops and weapons and other military equipment in the conflict zones while still ensuring deterrence for all parties.

In the case of Moldova, this will require demilitarizing the PMR (see below). In Georgia, the "partisan" groups will have to be reined in and their activities halted. An agreement in Nagorno-Karabakh will have to include reductions in the size of military forces along the former line of contact and on the postsettlement borders. The separatist area could retain a lightly armed local paramilitary police force.

To increase confidence between the parties, the international community should play a more active role in providing security guarantees. The deployment of observer missions (not necessarily peacekeeping forces) on the new front lines would be a valuable step. The UN mission in Georgia can serve as a model for such missions. UNOMIG functions reasonably well, fulfilling its mandate to monitor the activities of the Russian-led CIS peacekeeping operation, but its shortcomings (notably, a limited mandate and the erosion of local support) have loomed large because the operation is not embedded in a more positive wider context. The international community should also press for a reduction in the numbers of Russian peacekeeping troops while providing support for the logistics and supplies of the Russian forces that do remain. A reduced Russian military presence integrated fully with international observer missions would still help to deter a resumption of hostilities by either side.

Society-to-Society Links

Much of the progress toward a settlement of the Karabakh conflict has been generated by international pressure and cooperation among the highest political elites. The wider Armenian and Azerbaijani societies have been left out of the process, an omission that has done nothing to thaw the existing cold war between the parties, characterized by spiraling distrust, almost no contact, and enduring reliance on military tools.

The key to long-term settlement of all the conflicts between post-Soviet metropolitan and de facto states lies in warming the frozen climate that exists at all levels of those conflicts. Society-to-society links should be built at all levels between the conflicting parties: at the political level, between the elites who run the executive, legislative, judicial, and local branches of government; at the economic level, between business elites and local traders, who should be able to operate in a more open market; and at the social level, between educators, opinion makers, and students.

Isolated from a wider settlement process, such bridge building will have little effect. However, if it is embedded in a coordinated, multidimensional approach, the process of forging links between adversarial societies will form the foundation of an enduring settlement.

Economic Support

A settlement must also be rooted in an economic framework that helps to break down the criminalized political economies of the de facto states and end their economic isolation. The economic blockades against Nagorno-Karabakh and the CIS sanctions regime against Abkhazia must be lifted and economic cooperation and trade between adversaries initiated.

The political authorities in Tbilisi and Baku often look toward the example of economic cooperation between Moldova and the PMR for reasons *not* to lift the embargoes. But the Moldovan case illustrates only the need for economic cooperation to be part of a multidimensional approach; if economic cooperation is pursued alone, as in Moldova, it will only entrench the criminalization of the de facto state and sectors of the metropolitan state and undermine the metropolitan economy. The lifting of the blockades and trade restrictions must be accompanied by continued assistance from international financial institutions to the metropolitan states. Some of this assistance should be earmarked for the de facto state. Moreover, the metropolitan state should allow the de facto state to develop privatized relations with other states, along the lines developed by Taiwan.

In general, the provision of humanitarian support by the international community should not be biased toward any of the parties in these conflicts. At present, although assistance is provided to both the separatist and the metropolitan states, for good reasons the latter receive the lion's share. The de facto states should be better integrated into the international humanitarian network, especially in light of the problems they face. One of these problems is the departure of their younger and more highly skilled residents, who leave behind the older and more vulnerable members of the population. Another problem is that the separatist areas are breeding grounds for communicable diseases, such as drug-resistant tuberculosis. The international community must help the de facto states confront these challenges by offering more extensive assistance than it has provided to date.

■ ■ ■

The policy strands delineated above are like infinitive verbs that will have to be conjugated differently according to the particular needs of the different conflicts. An appropriate international mechanism must be created for each conflict. In each case, the European Union or the United Nations would assign a special representative to lead the settlement process (along the lines already set by the United Nations in Georgia and the European Union in the South Caucasus). The special representative would create a regional task force that would bring together the conflicting parties with major third parties, such as Russia, and international organizations and financial institutions. The costs of such coordination are mainly political, calculated in terms of the energy and attention expended by the European Union or the United Nations and their member-states in launching a process and sustaining it with high-level pressure and political visibility. To overcome the inertia of the status quo, the special representative, working through the regional task force, would need to create a sense of inevitability—that is, a sense that the process of conflict settlement spearheaded by the special representative is unstoppable, that the international community will not be swayed from its determination to achieve a lasting solution to each conflict.

WHERE TO START?

The prospects for progress toward lasting settlements in the Caucasus are mixed. Talks over Abkhazia remain blocked by the conflicting parties' divisions, as well as by differences among the third parties over how best to proceed. The settlement of the conflict with South Ossetia remains hostage to the resolution of the Georgian-Abkhaz conflict. The situation is more promising in the case of the Karabakh conflict, where the points agreed on in 2001 may serve—in a reworked presentation—as the basis for future negotiations. But any attempt to push for a comprehensive settlement in Azerbaijan must wait until the dust settles from the 2003 presidential elections, which marked the country's first change in executive power. Heydar Aliyev's son, Ilham, has to devote time and energy to firmly establishing himself in power in Baku before contemplating any new and ambitious approach to Nagorno-Karabakh. The Rose Revolution of November 2003, followed by the presidential elections in early 2004, brought a new, reformist team to power in Tbilisi, whose primary task is to restore some semblance of order and stability to Georgia's political and economic situation. This is a demanding task, and the authorities in Tbilisi are thus unlikely to launch bold or new policies toward either South Ossetia or Abkhazia in the near future, especially given the rise of a challenge to Georgian central power from Aslan Abashidze in the region of Ajaria. The international community, therefore, should first look not to the Caucasus but to Moldova as the place to launch a full-fledged international push for settlement.

The European Union is well positioned to take the lead in Moldova; in fact, it is increasingly doing so.[18] From Brussels' perspective, Moldova's importance will increase as the European Union enlarges. This small state is already a criminal gateway into

Europe for drugs, smuggled arms, and, in particular, illegal immigrants. Furthermore, Moldova has close ties with Romania, which is scheduled for EU membership in 2007. In 2002, the Moldovan parliament decided to allow dual citizenship, opening up the possibility that many Moldovan citizens may obtain Romanian citizenship—and thus access to the other EU member-states. Despite the OSCE's involvement, little progress has been made toward resolving the conflict between Moldova and Transnistria. Should the situation persist, the danger exists that Moldova will become a black hole on Europe's border, radiating instability externally while collapsing internally. The self-declared PMR is the center of gravity of all of Moldova's weaknesses. A major political kick-start is required to set in motion a comprehensive peace process. The European Union, working with Russia, is well placed to drive a strategy that would combine high-level political pressure with targeted economic assistance and a limited military observer presence.

The European Union can bring to bear a mixture of political and economic weight across the region that the OSCE cannot. Furthermore, the European Union's motivation to do so is greater than the OSCE's; indeed, the European Union urgently needs to launch a new dynamic in the region. Constant high-level political pressure is required to nudge the parties, and the PMR in particular, toward formal settlement of the conflict. The European Union's political and economic weight in its relations with Romania, Moldova, and Ukraine provide it with some leverage over the behavior of these states.

In addition, Russia's diplomatic weight in Moldova and Ukraine will be vitally important. The European Union could draw on the Russian peacekeeping forces already deployed in the conflict zone. These forces should be reduced and integrated into a new operation structured to fulfill a new mandate. The Russian peacekeepers should become military observers, working alongside observers from EU member-states.

A constellation of factors creates a situation that is pregnant with potential. The OSCE has developed a settlement package that has the support of the main external parties—Ukraine, Russia, and even the United States—through their leadership of the OSCE mission. The regional context is also favorable, with Romania in line for EU membership in 2007, and with Ukraine, Moldova, and even Belarus eager to forge closer ties with Brussels. Russia under President Vladimir Putin has never been so open to international involvement in the former Soviet Union, and for all its frustration with Brussels, Moscow is ready to develop a deeper political and security dialogue with the European Union and its member-states. At the same time, the European Union has started to consider the reality of the new borders and new neighbors that enlargement will bring. What is more, the costs of a new approach to Moldova are essentially political, with no military requirements except the deployment of a modestly sized observer mission.

The OSCE mission presented a "non-paper" in 2002 for a final settlement of the conflict, which would lead to Moldova becoming a federative republic and would accord significant rights to the PMR as a "state-territorial" unit.[19] For the first time in the history of the negotiations, which have stalled and restarted for more than a decade, an international consensus emerged: the draft agreement had the backing of Russia and Ukraine, as well as the United States, which has also taken a more prominent role in the negotiating process through its chairmanship of the OSCE mission. Moreover, Moldova's president, Vladimir Voronin, presented a proposal in February 2003 that called for redrafting the Moldovan constitution with Transnistrian participation. Such a revision of the constitution will require external support and expertise and, more widely, a comprehensive international push to sustain and complete the process, which could easily become obstructed by internal Moldovan differences and Transnistrian hardheadedness. A Russian proposal in November 2003 of a draft constitutional agreement caught the other mediators by surprise and demonstrated Moscow's enduring instinct for unilateral action. After some procrastination, Voronin refused to sign the draft because of its inherent weaknesses as a project to solve the conflict and because it was unpopular with significant sections of Moldovan society. Despite enduring obstacles, the pieces for a settlement still exist in Moldova; the European Union's role would be to integrate them and thus break the inertia that has set in over the past decade. Drawing on the general framework described above, a new EU-led approach to this conflict could have three strands: political, economic, and crisis management.

Political Strand

1. The aim of the EU approach at the political level would be to spearhead international engagement through the creation of a regional task force comprising the OSCE, Russia, Ukraine, and Moldova, as well as representatives from international financial institutions. The authorities of the PMR would also be invited to participate in the task force, so that their views could be taken into account and a forum created in which pressure could be placed on the PMR. The task force would provide strategic direction to the negotiations and a wide framework within which the policies of all the actors concerned could be coordinated.

2. Chaired jointly by the European Union and Russia, through special representatives, the regional task force would work to place political pressure on the Moldovan and PMR parties to agree on a new constitution regulating their relations. High-level visits to the region by Russian and European officials and efforts to give the settlement process high political and media visibility would create an impression of inevitability and would help bind together the various strands in the existing efforts by different elements of the international community.

3. Political pressure has to focus some attention on Ukraine, with the aim of persuading Ukraine to monitor carefully and effectively its border with the PMR, thereby putting a halt to regional smuggling. EU policy already seeks to reinforce all of Ukraine's borders. More attention and material support must be given to enhancing security along its border with the PMR.

4. The regional task force would act as a security guarantor for the implementation of the constitutional settlement agreement.

Economic Strand

1. As the European Union moves to develop its Wider Europe—New Neighborhood initiative, it must consider creating incentives to underpin any settlement reached in Moldova. The Stabilization and Association Process in the Balkans makes explicit use of future association with the European Union as leverage over states in that area. This example cannot be followed in the case of Moldova, as EU membership for Moldova is unfeasible for now; however, it might be possible to hold out the long-term prospect of Moldova, as a new EU neighbor, entering into some form of close association with the European Union.

2. At the same time, the political sensitivities of the PMR leadership, a section of which is deeply anti-Western, must be taken into account, and assurances given that their views will be heard and that the process of settlement and normalization will be slow and gradual.

3. The European Union should consider coordinating its policies toward Moldova with those of the International Monetary Fund and the World Bank to achieve optimal leverage. The latter two institutions suspended their activities in Moldova but have now resumed them. Were they to extend those activities to the PMR, the negotiation process could

create incentives for cooperative behavior from the separatist authorities.

Crisis Management Strand

1. There is no need for a military operation in Moldova; indeed, the area is already far too militarized. The security zone between Moldova and the PMR is full of peacekeeping forces and PMR "security forces" and "customs points." However, an EU-Russian military observer mission, larger in size than the present OSCE operation and endowed with formal rights and responsibilities, could be formed to replace the OSCE observer mission. Elements of Russian peacekeeping forces could participate alongside military observers from EU member-states.

2. The mandate of the military observer mission would be to demilitarize the conflict zone through the following actions:

   - providing additional material support to the Russian government in disposing of the arms stocks of the former Soviet 14th Army, thereby ensuring the swiftest possible fulfillment of the obligations undertaken at the Istanbul summit in 1999;

   - providing support to the PMR for the demobilization of its numerous "border guards," "customs officers," and "security forces" through the creation of a single unarmed force (to be called the Dnestr Force and to be modeled on the Kosovo Protection Corps) that will be based in the PMR and will draw from the local population;

   - monitoring not only the security zone but also the Dnestr Force and the joint border posts on the eastern border with Ukraine;

   - providing training and material support to a new corps of joint Moldovan-PMR border guards, who would be deployed on the PMR's border with Ukraine; and

- creating a new Joint Security Commission under the regional task force (in place of the Joint Control Commission) to meet on a weekly basis to monitor all developments in the security zone and on the borders, chaired jointly by Russia and the European Union, and including the OSCE, Moldova, the PMR, and Ukraine.

6

Conclusions

THE POST-SOVIET DE FACTO STATES have subsistence economies. They are riddled with crime. And they face severe external threats. In sum, they appear destined to collapse. But such a fate is not inevitable.

The de facto states have survived for a decade, and they seem sufficiently well entrenched to last another ten years. Their claim to statehood carries a logic that is difficult to overcome now that it has been launched. As the anthropologist Ann Maria Alonso noted: "Baptized with a name, space becomes national property, a sovereign patrimony fusing place, property, and heritage, whose perpetuation is secured by the state."[1] In their own view, the de facto states have already been playing in the game of states for ten years. The attributes of statehood, in particular internal sovereignty and empirical statehood, are no longer negotiable in practice. These states will hold out as long as they can. From their perspective, the status quo plays in their favor. Nonrecognition and international isolation are prices that they are willing to pay. The Abkhaz defense minister told me in July 2000: "How long will we have to wait? Ten, twenty, thirty years? Let it be, we will wait."[2] In a similar vein, the prime minister of Nagorno-Karabakh, Anushavan Danielyan, stated: "Nonrecognition does not affect Nagorno-Karabakh's existence, or its status as an independent state. . . . Nagorno-Karabakh is the same as Azerbaijan, but it is just not recognized!"[3] These de facto states are playing the long game, in which not losing means winning.

Any settlement will have to be based on the reality of the existence of self-declared states. Power sharing is not a workable or obvious solution, as it was in the Tajik civil war, as the separatist states have little desire to share power in a meaningful sense, have no sense of a shared destiny with the metropolitan states, and are in fact determined to exit the metropolitan states. The initial causes of the conflicts are less important now than this reality.

The international community, the metropolitan states, and international organizations have applied a number of policies ranging from outright hostility to limited engagement with the de facto states. The result has been a mixed bag of approaches with little coherence and no strategy. Neither Europe nor the international community as a whole can afford to continue pursuing piecemeal policies toward these conflicts that do little to advance their settlement. The stakes are high in strategic and regional security terms. These conflicts are driven not by primordial clashes or ancient hatreds; clearly identifiable and very modern processes sustain them. A key objective of this study has been to highlight these processes and to explore pressure points where international engagement may alter the status quo.

If the international community is to set these conflicts on the path toward settlement, it must create a new logic on the ground that addresses the dynamic processes driving the self-declared states. A five-pronged approach could do much to break the current inertia. Many elements of such an approach are already present in international policies toward these conflicts and the de facto states, but those elements are isolated from one another and applied inconsistently, with the result that they often contradict one another or work at cross-purposes. If they were combined in a coordinated international effort that had clear and limited objectives, they could overcome the inertia that grips the post-Soviet conflicts so tightly. The metropolitan states may object to the fudged solution proposed above, and with good reason: it will not restore their full sovereignty over lost territories. However, the losers of wars are rarely given appealing options. A solution that balances de facto with de jure sovereignty is the key to achieving a lasting settlement.

The conflicts will not resolve themselves, and the de facto states will not disappear of their own volition. Ten years after the Soviet collapse, the separatist states are deeply embedded in the post-Soviet world. In the absence of strategic coordination by the international community, the de facto states will still exist ten years from now. Even if a more cohesive international effort is forthcoming, they will not disappear entirely. But in the absence of such coordination, one can be sure that the former Soviet Union will be confirmed as a zone of strategic risk, emitting a constant pulse of instability while slowly collapsing internally.

Notes

1. INTRODUCTION

1. Reported in *Jamestown Monitor* 6, no. 224 (December 1, 2000).

2. Henceforth, for reasons of simplicity, these will be referred to as the PMR (or Transnistria), South Ossetia, Abkhazia, and Nagorno-Karabakh.

3. The term "state" being applied in this text to the unrecognized entities does not mean they should be recognized; it is a simplifying device to emphasize how the leaders of the separatist areas themselves interpret their objectives.

4. One early substantive work on the post-Soviet separatist states was Dov Lynch, "De Facto States and Security in the Former Soviet Union," written for the annual convention of the Association for the Study of Nationalities in New York, April 7, 2001.

5. Edward Walker, "No Peace, No War in the Caucasus: Secessionist Conflicts in Chechnya, Abkhazia and Nagorno-Karabakh," Occasional Paper, Strengthening Democratic Institutions Project (Cambridge, Mass.: Harvard University Center for Science and International Affairs, February 1998).

6. Charles King, "The Benefits of Ethnic War: Understanding Eurasia's Unrecognized States," *World Politics*, no. 53 (July 2001): 524–552.

7. On the notion of a de facto state, see Scott Pegg, *International Society and the De Facto State* (Aldershot: Ashgate, 1998), in which Pegg examines such de facto states as Eritrea, northern Cyprus, and Taiwan—states that exist, or existed, in empirical terms but have not been recognized by the international community.

8. See Dov Lynch, *Russian Peacekeeping Strategies in the CIS: The Cases of Moldova, Georgia and Tajikistan* (London: Royal Institute of International Affairs and Macmillan, 2000).

9. The notion is associated with the work of I. William Zartman, developed first in *Ripe for Resolution* (New York: Oxford University Press, 1989) and heavily debated since by a range of scholars, such as Jeffrey Rubin, Stephen Stedman, Marieke Kleiboer, and Richard Haass.

10. Parts of the research for this study were presented to the annual conference of the Association for the Study of Nationalities at Columbia University, April 6, 2001, and published in *World Today* 57, no. 8 (August 2001); *Managing Separatist States: A Eurasian Case Study,* Occasional Paper 32 (Paris: WEU Institute for Strategic Studies, 2001); and "Separatist States and Post-Soviet Conflicts," *International Affairs* 78, no. 4 (October 2002): 831–848.

11. From the cease-fire agreement of August 31, 1997, which was signed in Khasavyurt, until September–October 1999 and the start of the second Chechen war, Chechnya was a de facto state. The Khasavyurt agreement provided for Russia's withdrawal and for the signature of a treaty to be effected by December 2001—thereby suspending the status question for a period of five years. In the interim, presidential elections were held in Chechnya and the institutions of statehood declared, if not created, by Aslan Maskhadov. The Chechen Republic of Ichkeria severed most ties with Moscow and interpreted the end of the war and Khasavyurt as de facto recognition of its independence.

12. A similar point must be made regarding the nomenclature of these wars; the battle over toponyms is woven into them, and place-names (e.g., Shusha/Shushi and Sukhumi/Sukhum) are heavily disputed and highly significant. The choices made in this study do not reflect political bias toward one or the other conflicting party.

2. THE DE FACTO STATE: DEFINITION, ENVIRONMENT, AND EMERGENCE

1. This section draws from Dov Lynch, "The Tajik Civil War and Peace Process," *Civil Wars* 4, no. 4 (winter 2001): 49–72.

2. See *Human Rights Questions: HR Situations and Reports of the Special Rapporteurs and Representatives,* United Nations A/51/483/Add. 1 (October 24, 1996), prepared by Francis Deng for the Fifty-first Session of the General Assembly.

3. Shirin Akiner noted the stress placed on the Tajik identity in "Central Asia and the Tajik Civil War" (paper presented at the War Studies Eurasian Security Seminar, King's College London, February 28, 2001).

4. Pegg, *De Facto State*, 26. Prior to Pegg's work, de facto states had received attention in the form of short articles, mostly on the cases of Eritrea and Taiwan. However, there had been no systematic attempt to frame the question analytically or to treat the states comparatively.

5. Ibid., 5.

6. Gunnar Agathon Stolsvik, *The Status of the Hutt River Province (Western Australia): A Case Study in International Law* (Bergen, Norway: Bergen University, 2000), 29.

7. Alan James, "Sovereignty—a Ground Rule or Gibberish?" *Review of International Studies* 10 (1984): 16.

8. See discussion in Pegg, *De Facto State.*

9. See Kemal S. Shehadi, *Ethnic Self-Determination and the Break-up of States*, Adelphi Paper 283 (London: International Institute for Strategic Studies, 1993); Darel Paul, "Sovereignty, Survival and the Westphalian Blind Alley in International Relations," *Review of International Studies* 25, no. 2 (1999): 217–231; Oyrind Osterud, "The Narrow Gate: Entry to the Club of Sovereign States," *Review of International Studies* 23 (1997): 167–184; and James Mayall, *Nationalism and International Society* (Cambridge, U.K.: Cambridge Studies in International Relations, Cambridge University Press, 1990).

10. Michael Freeman, "The Right to Self-Determination in International Politics: Six Theories in Search of a Policy," *Review of International Studies* 25 (1999): 359.

11. This point is well made by Stuart and Anne-Marie Gardner, "Self-Determination in the Western Sahara: Legal Opportunities and Political Roadblocks," *International Peacekeeping* 7, no. 2 (summer 2000): 115–138.

12. Stanley Hoffmann, *Duties beyond Borders: On the Limits and Possibilities of Ethical International Politics* (Syracuse, N.Y.: Syracuse University Press, 1981), 34.

13. Mayall, *Nationalism*, 56.

14. On this point, see Pegg, *De Facto State.*

15. See discussion in J. D. B. Miller, "Sovereignty as a Source of Vitality for the State," *Review of International Studies* 12 (1986): 79–89.

16. Ibid., 82.

17. Alan James, "The Equality of States: Contemporary Manifestations of an Ancient Doctrine," *Review of International Studies* 18 (1992): 381.

18. James, "Sovereignty," 16.

19. See Pegg, *De Facto State*, 55–66.

20. M. Hassen, "Eritrean Independence and Democracy in the Horn of Africa," in Amare Tekle, ed., *Eritrea and Ethiopia: From Conflict to Cooperation* (Trenton, N.J.: Red Sea Press, 1994), cited in Pegg, *De Facto State*, 64.

21. In this respect, the Puntland State of Somalia in the northeast of Somalia might also be considered.

22. William Reno, *Somalia and Survival in the Shadow of the Global Economy*, Working Paper 100 (Oxford: Queen Elizabeth House, February 2003), 4; available at www2.qeh.ox.ac.uk.

23. Peggy Hoyle, "Somaliland: Passing the Statehood Test?" *Boundary and Security Bulletin* (autumn 2000): 80–91.

24. On the TRNC, see Nathalie Tocci, "Cyprus and the European Union: Catalysing Crisis or Settlement?" (unpublished paper, October 2001); C. H. Dodd, ed., *The Political, Social, and Economic Development of Northern Cyprus* (Huntingdon, U.K.: Eothen Press, 1993).

25. See, for example, Barry Posen, "The Security Dilemma and Ethnic Conflict," *Survival* 35 (spring 1993): 27–47; and Jack Snyder, "Introduction: Reconstructing Politics amidst the Wreckage of Empire," in Barnett R. Rubin and Jack Snyder, eds., *Post-Soviet Political Order: Conflict and State-Building* (London: Routledge, 1998), 1–13.

26. Stuart J. Kaufman, *Modern Hatreds: The Symbolic Politics of Ethnic War* (Ithaca, N.Y.: Cornell University Press, 2001).

27. Svante E. Cornell, *Autonomy and Conflict: Extraterritoriality and Separatism in the South Caucasus—Cases in Georgia* (Uppsala, Sweden: Uppsala University Department of Peace and Conflict Research, 2002).

28. Barnett R. Rubin, "Russian Hegemony and State Breakdown in the Periphery: Causes and Consequences of the Civil War in Tajikistan," in Rubin and Snyder, *Post-Soviet Political Order*, 128–161.

29. Thomas de Waal, *Black Garden: Armenia and Azerbaijan through Peace and War* (New York: New York University Press, 2003); see also Matthew Evangelista, *The Chechen Wars: Will Russia Go the Way of the Soviet Union?* (Washington, D.C.: Brookings Institution Press, 2003).

30. Joseph Stalin, *Marxism and the National and Colonial Question* (London: Lawrence & Wishart, 1936); see also the discussion in Graham Smith, "The Soviet State and Nationalities Policy," in Graham Smith, ed., *The Nationalities Question in the Post-Soviet States*, 2d ed. (London: Longman, 1996), 2–22.

31. See discussion in Ian Bremmer, "Reassessing Soviet Nationalities Theory," in Ian Bremmer and Ray Taras, eds., *Nations and Politics in the*

Soviet Successor States (Cambridge, U.K.: Cambridge University Press, 1993), 3–26.

32. See Ronald Grigor Suny, *The Revenge of the Past: Nationalism, Revolution, and the Collapse of the Soviet Union* (Stanford, Calif.: Stanford University Press, 1993).

33. Ibid., 85.

34. See also discussion in "Post-colonialism and Borderland Identities," in Graham Smith, Vivien Law, Andrew Wilson, Annette Bohr, and Edward Allworth, *Nation-Building in the Post-Soviet Borderlands: The Politics of National Identity* (Cambridge, U.K.: Cambridge University Press, 1998), 1–20.

35. This point is made by Olga Jourek, *Ethno-Political Conflicts in the Post-Communist Societies: Prospects for Resolution and Prevention in the Context of International Law*, Strengthening Democratic Institutions Project (Cambridge, Mass.: Harvard University Center for Science and International Affairs, September 1999), 58; see also Svante E. Cornell, "The Devaluation of the Concept of Autonomy: National Minorities in the Former Soviet Union," *Central Asian Survey* 18, no. 2 (1999): 185–196.

36. This point is well made in Cornell, "Devaluation of Autonomy."

37. Svante Cornell explores comprehensively the stimulating force of "autonomy" behind conflicts in the Caucasus in *Autonomy and Conflict: Ethnoterritoriality and Separatism in the South Caucasus—Cases in Georgia*, Report 61 (Stockholm: Uppsala University Department of Peace and Conflict Research, 2002).

38. Ibid.

39. See the discussion of this process in Shehadi, *Ethnic Self-Determination*, 23–31.

40. This point was made in a talk given at the London School of Economic and Political Science and Economics, March 1, 2001.

41. David D. Laitin and Ronald Grigor Suny, "Armenia and Azerbaijan: Thinking Way Out of Karabakh," *Middle East Policy* 7, no. 1 (October 1999): 149.

42. On the sources of this conflict, see the excellent special issue of *Accord* on the conflict, published by Conciliation Resources in London in September 1999; www.c-r.org/accord/geor-ab/accord7/index.shtml. Also see Suzanne Goldenberg, *Pride of Small Nations* (London: Zed Books, 1994), 81–115; Elizabeth Fuller, "Abkhazia on the Brink of Civil War?" *RFE/RL Research Reports*, September 4, 1992, 1–4; and John Colarusso, "Abkhazia," *Central Asian Survey*, January 14, 1995, 76.

43. See discussion in Bruno Coppieters, David Darchiashvili, and Natella Achaba, *Federal Practice: Exploring Alternatives for Georgia and Abkhazia* (Brussels: VUB Press, 2001); Bruno Coppieters, *Federalism and Conflict Resolution: Perspectives for the South Caucasus,* Discussion Paper (London: Chatham House, December 2001); and Bruno Coppieters, ed., *Contested Borders in the Caucasus* (Concord, Mass.: Paul and Company, 1996).

44. On these historical debates, see Smith, Law, Bohr, and Allworth, *Nation-Building in the Post-Soviet Borderlands,* 48–66.

45. Cornell, *Autonomy and Conflict,* 168–169.

46. See Evgenny M. Kozhokin, "Georgia-Abkhazia," in Jeremy Azrael and Emil Paid, eds., *U.S. and Russian Policy-Making with Respect to the Use of Force* (Santa Monica, Calif.: RAND Corporation, 1996); and also the discussion in Dov Lynch, *The Conflict in Abkhazia: Russian Peacekeeping Dilemmas* (London: Royal Institute of International Affairs, June 1998).

47. On sources and evolution of conflict, see Charles King, *The Moldovans: Romania, Russia, and the Politics of Culture* (Stanford, Calif.: Hoover Institution Press, 2000); Charles King, *Post-Soviet Moldova: A Borderland in Transition* (London: Royal Institute of International Affairs, 1995); and Vladimir Socor, "Creeping Putsch in Eastern Moldova," *RFE/RL Research Reports,* January 17, 1992.

48. Daria Fane, "Moldova: Breaking Loose from Moscow," in Ian Bremmer and Ray Taras, eds., *Nations and Politics in the Soviet Successor States* (Cambridge, U.K.: Cambridge University Press, 1993), 138–139.

49. See Nicholas Dima, *Moldova and the Transdnestr Republic* (Boulder, Colo.: East European Monographs, 2001), 43–60.

50. See excellent discussion of the process of forging a Moldovan nation in King, *The Moldovans,* 63–119.

51. Ibid., 132–133.

52. On the origins of this conflict, see also Stuart J. Kaufman, *Modern Hatreds: The Symbolic Politics of Ethnic War* (Ithaca, N.Y.: Cornell University Press, 2001), 129–164.

53. S. J. Kaufman argues that the conflict, which has encompassed economic and political aspects, has been broadly ethnic. See "Spiralling to Ethnic War," *International Security* (fall 1996): 108–138. It is undeniable that ethnic issues sparked off this conflict, yet it seems that political and economic contradictions underlie the fundamental conflict between the region and the central government.

54. See discussion in King, *Post-Soviet Moldova,* 21–23.

55. King, *The Moldovans,* 184.

56. Ibid., 185.

57. Information gathered from interviews by author in Chisinau and Tiraspol, May 1998.

58. For an overview of these activities, see Michael Lucas, "Russia and the CIS: The Role of the CSCE," *Helsinki Monitor* 5, no. 4 (1994).

59. Interviews by the author with military members of the mission to Moldova, May 1998.

60. Ibid.

61. See www.osce.org/moldova.

62. See discussion in Bruno Coppieters and Michael Emerson, *Conflict Resolution for Moldova and Transdniestria through Federalisation?* CEPS Policy Brief 25 (Brussels: Centre for European Policy Studies: August 2002); http://shop.ceps.be/free/126.pdf.

63. On this conflict, its sources, evolution, and consequences, Thomas de Waal has done by far the best work; see de Waal's *Black Garden.* See also David D. Laitin and Ronald Grigor Suny, "Armenia and Azerbaijan," 145–176, and Larry Minear and Neil MacFarlane, *Humanitarian Action and Politics: The Case of Nagorno-Karabakh,* Thomas J. Watson Jr. Institute for International Studies Occasional Paper 25 (Providence, R.I.: Brown University, 1997).

64. De Waal, *Black Garden,* 126.

65. Ibid., 184–183.

66. See the discussion of histories and myths in Kaufman, *Modern Hatreds,* 53.

67. Proceedings of the Committee on the Caucasus, cited in de Waal, *Black Garden,* 129–130. De Waal offers an explanation for the change of mind.

68. See *Report on the Conflict in Nagorno-Karabakh* (Council of Europe, Parliamentary Assembly Doc. 7182, October 17, 1994).

3. THE LOGIC DRIVING THE SEPARATIST STATES

1. Interview by author, Chisinau, July 13, 2000.

2. Interview by author, Tbilisi, August 7, 2000.

3. Interview by author, Tiraspol, July 11, 2000.

4. Ardzinba interview in *Abkhazia Newsletter* 2, no. 24 (December 19, 1999).

5. See Inal Kashig, "Abkhazia: Veterans Challenge President," *IWPR Caucasus Reporting Service* no. 187 (2003).

6. Jaba Devdariani, "South Ossetian Leader Tightens Control over Breakaway Georgian Province," *Eurasia Insight,* July 24, 2003.

7. Alexandre Kukhianidze, *Organized Crime and Smuggling through Abkhazia and Its Impact on Georgian-Abkhaz Conflict Resolution* (unpublished paper, Georgia Office of the American University Transnational Crime and Corruption Center, Washington, D.C., 2003).

8. Interview by author, Sukhumi, July 22, 2000.

9. For a comprehensive overview of the economic situation in Abkhazia, see UNDP Working Group III, *UN Needs Assessment Mission to Abkhazia, Georgia* (New York: United Nations Development Program, March 1998).

10. Interview with the minister of economics and reconstruction, Stepanakert, August 20, 2000.

11. As the mayor of the showcase village of Karintak admitted, people are at the end of their tether: "We were patient during the war. We were patient during the years after the war. But now the government must do something about this."

12. See discussion in King, "The Benefits of Ethnic War," 524–552.

13. Interview with Valery Zhed, minister of economics, Tiraspol, July 2000.

14. Interview by author, Tiraspol, July 14, 2000.

15. On the difference between the declaratory and the constitutive approach, see discussion in Michael Ross Fowler and Julie Marie Bunce, "What Constitutes the Sovereign State?" *Review of International Studies* 22 (1996): 400–402.

16. Interview by author, Tiraspol, July 11, 2000. In fact, de facto states may have a status in international law, not as such but as a nonsovereign state, and may be held accountable.

17. Interview by author, Sukhumi, July 25, 2000.

18. Interview by author, Sukhumi, July 20, 2000.

19. Interview by author, Stepanakert, August 16, 2000.

20. Interview by author, Sukhumi, July 20, 2000.

21. Interview by author, Sukhumi, July 20, 2000.

22. Interview by author, Tiraspol, July 14, 2000.

23. Interview with S. Aragian, Yerevan, August 11, 2000.

24. See the collection of all agreements reached in this conflict, *Basic Documents in Pridnestrovyan Conflict Resolution* (Kiev: Friedrich Ebert Stiftung Bureau for Cooperation with Ukraine, 2000).

25. Valery Litskai, unpublished paper (February 2000).

26. This has been a major sticking point in Georgian-Abkhaz talks on new constituent relations.

27. Interview by author, Sukhumi, July 31, 2000.

28. Interview by author, Sukhumi, July 28, 2000.

29. Interview by author, Sukhumi, July 28, 2000.

30. Interview by author, Stepanakert, August 24, 2000.

31. Interview in Stepanakert, August 17, 2000.

32. Interview by author, Sukhumi, July 25, 2000.

33. Arda Inal-Ipa, "Questions of Land and Other Problems in Abkhaz-Georgia Conflict Resolution," in Paula Garb, Arda Inal-Ipa, and Paata Zakareishvili, eds., *Aspects of the Georgian-Abkhazian Conflict* (Irvine, Calif.: University of California, August 1999).

34. Interview with the Abkhaz defense minister, Sukhumi, July 31, 2000.

35. Ibid.

36. Interviews with such teachers in Mardakert, Nagorno-Karabakh, October 1998.

37. On these notions, see Smith, Law, Bohr, and Allworth, *Nation-Building,* 13–17.

38. See the historical textbooks published by the Transnistrian State University, such as *Dubossary—Bleeding Wound of Pridnestrovye* (1999) and *Pridnestrovyan Conflict—Historical, Demographic, and Political Aspects* (1998).

39. From "War-Making and State-Making as Organized Crime," in Peter Evans, D. Rueschemeyer and T. Skocpol, eds., *Bringing the State Back In* (New York: Cambridge University Press, 1985), cited in Hugh Griffiths, "A Political Economy of Ethnic Conflict: Ethno-Nationalism and Organized Crime," *Civil Wars* 2, no. 2 (summer 1999): 56–73.

40. See public statements by a number of political and social groups tied to the ministry in November 1999 declaring that the withdrawal of Russian troops from the left bank would "leave the Transnistrian people face to face with revanchist forces," reported by Infotag (www.infotag.md), December 22, 1999.

41. Interview by author, Stepanakert, August 15, 2000.

42. Interview with Melkoumian, Stepanakert, August 24, 2000.

43. Interview with Melkoumian, Stepanakert, August 17, 2000.

44. Cornell, *Autonomy and Conflict,* 47.

45. This point emerged from a discussion held in London with Bruno Coppietiers in November 2000.

46. See the discussion in chapter 1 of Yelena Kalyuzhnova and Dov Lynch, eds., *The Euro-Asian World: A Period of Transition* (London: Macmillan, 2000).

47. Interview by author, Tiraspol, July 11, 2000.

48. Interview by author, Sukhumi, July 20, 2000.

49. Interview by author, Stepanakert, August 17, 2000.

50. Interview by author, Stepanakert, August 15, 2000.

51. This correlates with some of Paul Collier's findings on the greed-and-grievance balance in civil wars, but it also indicates the interrelationship between the different explanations. See, for example, Paul Collier and Anke Hoeffler, "Greed and Grievance in Civil War" (October 21, 2001), and Paul Collier, "Doing Well Out of War" (April 10, 1999), both available at www.worldbank.org/research/conflict/papers/econagenda.htm.

52. This retreat to an "economy of subsistence and survival" in Abkhazia is noted in UNDP Working Group III, *Assessment Mission Abkhazia* (1998).

53. Interview by author, Stepanakert, August 21, 2000.

54. Interview by author, Karintak, Nagorno-Karabakh, August 18, 2000.

55. Interview by author, Sukhumi, July 23, 2000.

56. Pastukhov, April 18, 2001, reported by Infotag.

57. King, "Benefits of Ethnic War."

58. Bushulyak, interview by author, Chisinau, July 13, 2000.

59. Paata Zakareishvili, "Political Responsibility and Perspectives for Conflict Resolution in Georgia-Abkhazia," in Natella Akaba, ed., *Abkhazia-Georgia: Obstacles on the Path to Peace* (Sukhumi, 2000), 24–29.

60. Paata Zakareishvili, "An Open Wound," *IWPR Caucasus Reporting Service*, no. 15 (London: Institute for War and Peace Reporting, January 2000).

61. The following section draws from my article "Peacekeeping Dilemmas and Euro-Asian Conflicts," in Lynch and Kalyuzhnova, eds., *The Euro-Asian World.* For a complete examination of Russian peacekeeping, see Lynch, *Russian Peacekeeping Strategies towards the CIS.*

62. Information gathered from interviews by the author in Chisinau and Tiraspol, May 1998.

63. See discussion in Lynch, *The Conflict in Abkhazia.*

64. Notes drawn from tours of the peacekeeping operations in the PMR and in Abkhazia with UNOMIG in July 2000.

65. The numerical strength of the peacekeeping forces stands at 1,720 men (446 Russian, 779 PMR, and 495 Moldovan).

66. This discussion of Russian peacekeeping draws from Dov Lynch, "Post-imperial Peacekeeping, Russia in the CIS," *IFS Info* (Norwegian Institute for Defense Studies), April 2003.

67. Interviews with members of the OSCE mission in Moldova in May 1998 and July 2000.

68. A point highlighted to me by members of the OSCE mission in June 1997. See also S. Neil MacFarlane, Larry Minear, and S. D. Shenfield, *Armed Conflict in Georgia: A Case Study in Humanitarian Action and Peace-keeping,* Occasional Paper 21 (Providence, R.I.: Thomas J. Watson Jr. Institute for International Studies, 1996).

4. The Security Impact of the Separatist States

1. Ghia Nodia, "The Conflict in Abkhazia: National Projects and Political Circumstances," in Bruno Coppieters, Ghia Nodia, and Yury Anchabadze, eds., *Georgians and Abkhazians: The Search for a Peace Settlement* (Brussels: VUB Press, 1998).

2. See discussion in Evgeny Polyakov, *Changing Trade Patterns after Conflict Resolution in the South Caucasus* (Washington, D.C.: World Bank, 2000).

3. Cited in MacFarlane, Minear, and Shenfield, *Armed Conflict in Georgia,* 17.

4. Cited by Anatoly Kuprianov, "Tensions Grow in Stepanakert," *Caucasus Report* (Institute for War and Peace Reporting), no. 59, November 24, 2000.

5. Ermolai Adzhindzhal, "On One Aspect of the Informational Blockade of Abkhazia," in *The Role of International Organizations in the Process of Post-conflict Peace-Building in Abkhazia* (Sukhumi: United Nations Abkhazian Association [UNAA], October 1996).

6. See the excellent analysis of this question by Catherine Dale, *The Dynamics and Challenges of Ethnic Cleansing: The Georgian-Abkhaz Case* (Geneva: UN High Commissioner for Refugees, August 1997), available from www.unhcr.ch through Refworld.

7. Polyakov, *Changing Trade Patterns*, 6–7.

8. See report on Infotag, November 8, 1999.

9. Nickolae Andranic, cited on Infotag, April 7, 1999.

10. William Hill, June 5, 1999, reported by Basa-Press News Agency (www.basa.md).

5. WAYS OUT

1. Pegg, *De Facto State*, 177–181. See also Pegg, "The Taiwan of the Balkans? The De Facto State Option for Kosovo," *Southeast European Politics* 1, no. 2 (December 2000): 90–100.

2. On the causes of these wars, see James Hughes, "Chechnya: The Causes of a Protracted Post-Soviet Conflict," *Civil Wars* 4, no. 4 (winter 2001): 11–48.

3. See Shehadi, *Ethnic Self-Determination*.

4. Haris Silajdzic, "The Dayton Peace Accord—a Treaty That Is Not Being Implemented," *Bosnia Report*, nos. 13-14 (December 1999–February 2000).

5. See also Susan Woodward, "Bosnia and Herzegovina—How Not to End a Civil War," in Barbara F. Walker and Jack Snyder, eds., *Civil Wars: Insecurity and Intervention* (New York: Columbia University Press, 1999), 73–115.

6. See Andrew March and Rudra Sil, *The "Republic of Kosova" (1989–98) and the Resolution of Ethno-Separatist Conflict: Rethinking "Sovereignty" in the Post–Cold War Era* (Philadelphia: University of Pennsylvania, Browne Centre for International Politics, January 1999).

7. See www.mfa.gov.yu/YugFrameset.htm.

8. See "Report of the Secretary General on Mission of Good Offices in Cyprus" (UN Security Council, S/2003/398, April 1, 2003); available on www.cyprus-un-plan.org/UN.pdf.

9. On this, see Thomas Diez, *Last Exit to Paradise? The EU, the Cyprus Conflict, and the Problematic "Catalytic Effect"* (Copenhagen: Copenhagen Peace Research Institute, June 2000); and Nathalie Tocci, "Cyprus and the European Union: Catalysing Crisis or Settlement?" (unpublished paper, October 2001).

10. See *Basic Documents in Pridnestrovyan Conflict Resolution*.

11. On an EU operation, see Dov Lynch, *Russia Faces Europe*, Chaillot Paper no. 60 (Paris: EU Institute for Security Studies, 2003).

12. On the evolution of the talks and the positions adopted by the parties and the mediators, see de Waal, *Black Garden.*

13. For an overview, see Laitin and Suny, "Armenia and Azerbaijan," 145–176.

14. For a discussion of recent developments, see Thomas de Waal, *Crossing the Line: Reflections on the Nagorno-Karabakh Peace Process* (London: Conciliation Resources Paper, May 2001); and *Negotiations on Nagorno-Karabakh: Where Do We Go from Here?* (Cambridge, Mass.: Caspian Studies Program, Harvard University School of Government, April 23, 2001).

15. Timothy D. Sisk, *Power Sharing and International Mediation in Ethnic Conflicts* (Washington, D.C.: United States Institute of Peace Press, 1997).

16. The Caucasus Stability Pact, put forward by the private Brussels-based Centre for European Policy Studies in 2000, sought to square this circle by calling for the creation of a European-style security system in the Caucasus that would provide a framework of shared institutions and expectations, as well as security guarantees, in which various forms of power sharing could be built throughout the region and especially between the metropolitan and de facto states. See Sergiu Celac, Michael Emerson, and Nathalie Tocci, *A Stability Pact for the Caucasus: A Consultative Document of the CEPS Task Force on the Caucasus* (Brussels: CEPS, 2000).

17. David D. Laitin and Ronald Grigor Suny develop an interesting proposal to solve the conflict over Nagorno-Karabakh from which some of the following discussion draws inspiration; see "Armenia and Azerbaijan."

18. Much of the following section draws from Lynch, *Russia Faces Europe.*

19. "Negotiations Process on Transdniestrian Settlement Restarts in Chisinau," OSCE press release, August 23, 2002; www.osce.org/news/generate.php3?news_id=2663&uid=2.

6. CONCLUSIONS

1. Ann Maria Alonso, "The Politics of Space, Time and Substance: State Formation, Nationalism and Ethnicity," *Annual Review of Anthropology* 23 (1994): 379–405.

2. Interview by author, Sukhumi, July 31, 2000.

3. Interview by author, Stepanakert, August 15, 2000.

Index

About the Author

Dov Lynch is a research fellow at the European Union Institute for Security Studies, an EU agency launched in January 2002 to provide policy expertise for the European Union's European Security and Defence Policy. At the EU Institute, Lynch directs research on security developments concerning Russia and the former Soviet Union; he devotes particular attention to developing an EU strategy for the South Caucasus and to the European Union's strategic partnership with Russia.

Lynch graduated in Soviet Studies from Yale and has a doctorate in international relations from St. Antony's College, University of Oxford. He has a tenured lectureship at the Department of War Studies, King's College London, and has been a research fellow at St. Antony's College and at the Royal Institute of International Affairs, Russia and Eurasia Programme. His major publications include *Russia Faces Europe* (2003) and *Russian Peacekeeping Strategies towards the CIS* (2000), and he coedited *Energy in the Caspian Region* (2002) and *The Euro-Asian World: A Period of Transition* (2000). His articles have appeared in *International Affairs*, the *Washington Quarterly*, *World Today*, and *European Security*.

United States Institute of Peace

The United States Institute of Peace is an independent, nonpartisan federal institution created by Congress to promote the prevention, management, and peaceful resolution of international conflicts. Established in 1984, the Institute meets its congressional mandate through an array of programs, including research grants, fellowships, professional training, education programs from high school through graduate school, conferences and workshops, library services, and publications. The Institute's Board of Directors is appointed by the President of the United States and confirmed by the Senate.

Chairman of the Board: Chester A. Crocker
Vice Chairman: Seymour Martin Lipset
President: Richard H. Solomon
Executive Vice President: Harriet Hentges
Vice President: Charles E. Nelson

Board of Directors

Chester A. Crocker (Chairman), James R. Schlesinger Professor of Strategic Studies, School of Foreign Service, Georgetown University

Seymour Martin Lipset (Vice Chairman), Hazel Professor of Public Policy, George Mason University

Betty F. Bumpers, Founder and former President, Peace Links, Washington, D.C.

Holly J. Burkhalter, Advocacy Director, Physicians for Human Rights, Washington, D.C.

Charles Horner, Senior Fellow, Hudson Institute, Washington, D.C.

Stephen D. Krasner, Graham H. Stuart Professor of International Relations, Stanford University

Marc E. Leland, Esq., President, Marc E. Leland & Associates, Arlington, Va.

Mora L. McLean, Esq., President, Africa-America Institute, New York, N.Y.

María Otero, President, ACCION International, Boston, Mass.

Daniel Pipes, Director, Middle East Forum, Philadelphia, Pa.

Barbara W. Snelling, former State Senator and former Lieutenant Governor, Shelburne, Vt.

Harriet Zimmerman, Vice President, American Israel Public Affairs Committee, Washington, D.C.

Members ex officio
Lorne W. Craner, Assistant Secretary of State for Democracy, Human Rights, and Labor

Michael M. Dunn, Lieutenant General, U.S. Air Force; President, National Defense University

Douglas J. Feith, Under Secretary of Defense for Policy

Richard H. Solomon, President, United States Institute of Peace (nonvoting)

Engaging Eurasia's Separatist States

This book is set in New Baskerville; the display type is Optima. Hasten Design Studio designed the book's cover; Mike Chase designed the interior. Helene Y. Redmond made up the pages. The text was proofread by Karen Stough. The index was prepared by Sonsie Conroy. The book's editor was Nigel Quinney.